but why don't we go to war?

but why don't we go to war?

Finding Jesus' Path to Peace

SUSAN MARK LANDIS

HERALD PRESS
Scottdale, Pennsylvania
Waterloo, Ontario

Library of Congress Cataloging-in-Publication Data
Landis, Susan Mark, 1958-
    But why don't we go to war? : finding Jesus' path to peace / Susan Mark
Landis.
        p.   cm.
    Includes bibliographical references.
    ISBN 0-8361-3647-0
    1. Peace—Religious aspects—Christianity—Study and teaching.
2. Mennonites—Doctrines—Study and teaching. 3. Christian education of
children. 4. Christian education of teenagers. 5. Christian
education—Home training. I. Title.
BT736.4.L28   1993
261.8'73'07—dc20   93-10849
                                                                              CIP

The paper used in this publication is recycled and meets the minimum re-
quirements of American National Standard for Information Sciences—Per-
manence of Paper for Printed Library Materials, ANSI Z39.48-1984.

Credits for art, used by permission: cover illustration and Pontius' Puddle
strips by Joel Kauffmann; page 29, needlepoint by Liz Wenger; 49,
anonymous engraving of Menno Simons from late 1600s; 68, engraving of
Dirk Willems by Jan Luyken, from *Martyrs Mirror*; Maximilianus on 118 and
the thatching on 159 are by Allan Eitzen, from *Coals of Fire*, Herald Press;
195, art by Käthe Kollwitz, from St. Etienne Gallery, formerly of New York.
The Bible is quoted or adapted, used by permission, all rights reserved, and
unless otherwise indicated is from the *New Revised Standard Version Bible*,
copyright 1989, by the Division of Christian Education of the National
Council of the Churches of Christ in the USA. Other quoted matter is
credited in the notes. Permission is hereby granted to copy verses, posters,
and graphics for local group or family use.

Dedicated to Dennis, Laura, and Joel,
my companions on the path to peace

**If only you had known this day
the way that leads to peace!**

—*Jesus* (Luke 19:41, REB)

**If we are to reach real peace in this world, . . .
we shall have to begin with the children.**

—*Mahatma Gandhi*

Contents

Foreword

During the war in the Persian Gulf, our daughter Beth's third-grade class at school wrote letters to U.S. soldiers in Saudi Arabia. The letters were innocent enough in content, expressing curiosity about food, weather, and landscape. Yet millions of North American children participated in similar activities and said their painful good-byes to family members called to military duty. Thus the war itself became a giant civic lesson on the need to use violence to resolve difficult problems.

This lesson permeates our consciousness when our countries are at war, and it continues to be assumed in our public life even during times of relative peace. Our nations expend enormous resources in money, talent, and spirit for war. Thereby they reinforce this assumption that violence is necessary and respectable. Thousands of times daily, this is reaffirmed on TV and movie screens, creating a formidable challenge to all who would follow and teach Christ's way of peace and reconciliation.

But Why *Don't We Go to War?* recognizes the enormity of the challenge. Landis sees in the task of teaching peace to youth a journey that encompasses all of life and all stages of life. This is not a book to be given to youth in the hopes that they will make private commitments to become peacemakers. Instead, parents and children, grandparents and siblings, all are invited to walk together, each taking further steps along the way of Jesus.

Recognizing the power and seductiveness of violence in our culture, Landis prescribes peace teaching accompanied by example and experience, as well as by consistency between actions and words. Learning, living, and teaching Christ's way of peace is thus a task for the whole church. If we are not striving to live out these values in our day-to-day relationships, we cannot teach or preach peace and justice.

Teaching peace is an intentional task. Just as we are intentional about teaching our children to read, to swim, or to ride a bike, so we must be intentional about teaching Christ's way of peace. We know the many ways in which our society promotes violent solutions to conflict. This task therefore requires strong commitment and practical skills. Both of these are provided in good measure throughout the book.

The dialogical format encourages parents and youth to talk with one another about war, peace, and faith. Whether we follow the script or freely depart from it, the book engages us in lively and serious dialogue with the biblical stories and with one another. As we join in the conversation, we become a part of the movement of God among us.

—*Titus Peachey*
Linda Gehman Peachey

Preface

I began this project to help Mennonite junior youths discover their peace heritage and in the process rediscovered my own community of faith. Without the help and encouragement of my sisters and brothers in the church, this project would have been less complete. I want to express thanks to the following.

With a questionnaire I asked many friends how they developed their peace beliefs. Good ideas came from Marie Beechy, Don Blosser, Carol Gamber, Charlie Geiser, Susan Goering, Joan Kauffman, Ted Koontz, Evelyn Kreider, Melvin Leidig, Sarah Miller, Cheryl Neuenschwander, Weldon Nisly, Linda Gehman Peachey, Gene Stoltzfus, Roy Umble, and Pearl Zehr.

Then I began circulating rough drafts for comments. Many people gave of themselves to make this manuscript more workable, accurate, and helpful: Lois Barrett, Atlee Beechy, Sue Burkholder, Tamara and Lucinda and Steve Gill, Ray and Wilma Gingerich, Cheryl Hershberger, Kathy McGinnis, Nancy Nussbaum, Judy Schrag, and Kathy and Wendy Smucker.

I especially benefited from the help of Daniel Schipani, Christian Education professor at Associated Mennonite Biblical Seminaries, and from his Educating for Peace and Justice class of spring 1992. Daniel took a rough idea and encouraged me to develop it into a true educational tool. This text is full of learning he willingly gave.

I entered this project as a novice, and I thank S. David Garber, my editor at Herald Press, for his patience and diligence. His knowledge of theology and Mennonite writings made this book more precise and complete.

Several other mentors have enriched my life, such as John Stoner, Lois Kenagy, Sue Clemmer Steiner, Gene Stoltzfus, and Ray Gingerich. I thank them for helping me discern my calling to be a peace and justice educator and begin to understand that there is no peace without justice. I continue learning what it means to be a peace and justice educator as my gifts are used in Ohio and beyond.

I have been loved and supported by many. My parents, George and Arlene Mark, brought me up in a peace tradition and over the years encouraged me in seeking peace. My congregation, Oak Grove Mennonite of Smithville, Ohio, nurtured and invigorated me as I began my ministry of peace and justice education. In December of 1992, my church invited me to join a Christian Peacemaker Team trip to Haiti and provided necessary financial and family support. That experience deepened my understanding of Jesus' command to "let the oppressed go free." Many Oak Grove women have cared for my children when I went to meetings or gave peace workshops. I especially thank Cheryl Neuenschwander, who regularly gave of her Thursdays so I could write this book. I find joy in being a member of the Pathfinders' Sunday school class.

I thank Hildy Amstutz for first asking the question, "How do we teach peace to our children?" and Winston Gerig for wondering what was stopping me from writing a book.

To Dennis, my husband and friend, and to our children, Laura and Joel, I dedicate this book. May we together continue our journey on the path of God's peace.

Session Summaries

But *why* don't we go to war?

Session 1. Jesus Came to Bring Peace
We don't go to war because we follow Jesus. Jesus came to bring peace and help others. If we want to follow Jesus, we will do the same.

Session 2. God's Children Love Enemies
We don't go to war because Jesus taught us to love. When we love our enemies, we are sharing God's love and are known as God's children.

Session 3. We Trust God Alone
We don't go to war because we do not rely on governments and their armed forces to save us from enemies. We place our trust in God alone.

Session 4. Peace Is God's Vision
We don't go to war because God's ideal, already in the Old Testament, is a peaceable kingdom.

Session 5. God Created All Peoples

We don't go to war because God created all peoples, and because Jesus lived, died, and was raised to save all peoples and teach them to love each other.

Session 6. We Make Peace

We don't go to war because we choose to follow Jesus' way of peace and spread more love and justice in the world.

Introduction

For Youth

Have you ever wondered . . .

Why Jesus tells us to love our enemies,
but the government tells us to go to war against them?

Who had the vision for peace in the Old Testament?

Whether it really works to return love for hate?

How to get along with people different from you?

How we can make peace?

If you ponder such puzzles, then this book and the interviews with peace models are created for you! Here you will discover answers to these questions and many more. When you read this book together with adults who care about you, all of you will learn more about following Jesus' path of peace.

Don't think you have to do all the learning! Adults also

need to find the path to peace. God expects them to continue searching out ways to live more like Jesus and to teach those ideas to the next generation.

In six sessions this book answers the question, "But *why* don't we go to war?" Each session has two conversations for at least two persons, you and an adult. It also has a story of how a peacemaker made peace and an interview with a present-day peacemaker. With each conversation are prayers and an occasional exciting biblical drama.

The conversations between you and an adult are times for you both to think and search for answers to tough questions about war and peace. In your lines, you'll often find: *Youth: (May respond).* This invites you to stop reading and take a few minutes to ask or answer a question and give your ideas.

At other points in the session, if you have thoughts you want to talk about, just stop reading and ask. If you have many things to discuss, you might save the rest of that reading for a different time. It is important for you to understand these ideas well enough to explain them to someone else and to live them out.

How you live matters to God. That's why I wrote this book, so you can understand the Bible and God's path to peace better. As you grow older, you will have more and more opportunities to decide whether or not you want to follow Jesus and the way of peace.

Maybe you've already had some chances. If you were in school during the Persian Gulf War, you might have been uncomfortable. My daughter, Laura, then in kindergarten, came home one day with a question. Every day before the class recited the pledge of allegiance, the teacher would say, "Stand up straight for the soldiers!"

Laura wondered if she should sit down when her teacher said that. Should she wear a yellow ribbon or draw flag pictures? She was scared to talk to her teacher about these things.

This is when parents or an adult friend should help. I

talked to her teacher and explained why Laura was uncomfortable. Even though the teacher didn't agree with our ideas, she understood Laura better and tried to help her feel more comfortable.

If you're sure what you think, you'll feel more at ease around others who have ideas different from yours. This book will help you better understand Jesus' reasons for telling us to love our enemies instead of going to war to kill them. At the back of the book is a "Youth Reading List" suggesting readings to go with each session. You may find some of these books in your church library. If not, ask your parents or teacher for help.

I hope you have a good time with this adventure. Maybe you'll want to make some special food to eat while you do the conversations, or decorate the room where you go through the readings.

I'd like to hear about your study, whether you send a letter or pictures or comics. I especially want to hear about a time you made peace. You can send your ideas to me along with your parents' evaluation from the end of the book, in care of Herald Press, 616 Walnut Ave., Scottdale, PA 15683.

Welcome to Jesus' path to peace! It will not always be easy, but it will be exciting. May you and your parents travel with God.

For Adults

This book is the result of my questions about how to pass on our Mennonite peace heritage to our children. My own childhood learnings can be directly traced to family reading sessions with *Coals of Fire*, by Elizabeth Hershberger Bauman (see Bibliography). How can we help our junior youths link our peacemaking stories to faith in God, Bible knowledge, and a life of justice? A beginning answer is in your hands.

Parts of the Book

Six sessions answer the question, "But *why* don't we go to war?" Adult-youth conversations form the core of each session. They appeal to our desire to better understand the Bible and its peace teachings. Using our minds this way helps us base our faith and theology on the Bible. Each conversation ends with a prayer, reminding us that our journey toward peace draws our souls closer to God's ways. In addition, the end of the book contains biblical dramas of unfamiliar passages.

Each session then has a story which captures how Christians have peacefully dealt with violence. Such memories give us courage and present us with role models from the past. Contemporary peacemakers telling their stories provide living role models. To change our ways, to take the stand to be peacemakers, we must engage our hearts as well as our minds. You may include suitable songs about peace. Projects (listed together in appendix 3) encourage us to take the next step and use our feet as a family on the path of God's peace.

Perhaps you are gasping for air and thinking, All that in one sitting with my energetic junior youths? Maybe on a flashy video, but not perched on the davenport reading a book!

Rest assured, this is not a marathon to see who can cram the most knowledge into a youth's head in the shortest amount of time. Let's look at each of these parts individually and then consider options for your time together.

Helps for Parents

Although you probably bought this book to teach your junior youths, it has also been designed to help *you* on the journey. If they are the students, then you must be the teacher! Like many other parents, you may be uncertain what to teach your youths or what you yourself believe. By preparing for each session and utilizing the helps, you will enrich the learning for yourself and for your junior youths.

By the time youth have reached late elementary school,

they are aware that parents don't have all the answers. Perhaps they are even sarcastic when you try to teach them the "right way." If you are willing to admit that you continue to strive to understand the way of God's peace in your own life, that you stumble and fall, your junior youths will more likely be willing to walk beside you. But if they see *you* as deciding from a position of authority that the peace stand is something *they must* learn and live by, they may rebel. Be clear that you are traveling the path together.

Each session has a brief summary which wraps up an answer to our basic question, "But *why* don't we go to war?" All the Bible verses used in the session are listed so you can meditate on them during your own separate devotion time. All parts of the conversations include a short explanation of the story and the faith focus to help you direct your thoughts as you prepare to teach your youth.

But the most important help you will find is "Notes for Parents." These push you to think over your own life and faith. They will deepen the learnings introduced to the youths and encourage further adult searching. At the back of this volume, Appendixes, Notes, Youth Reading List, and Bibliography mention books and relate many of them to specific sessions.

Bible Memory Verses

Each of the six sessions has a core verse for the entire family to memorize. The verse appears at the beginning of the session and within each reading. Copy the verses on cards and leave them in strategic places around the house: on the bathroom mirror, over the kitchen sink, on the back door, on the bulletin board. With the verses constantly before you, memorizing them will be simple. Learning to live by the verses will take much longer!

You have permission to copy verses, posters, and graphics for local group or family use.

Youth-Adult Conversations

These conversations are the nucleus of presenting peace understandings of the Bible and Jesus' way. The youth questions, the adult answers. This programmed dialogue may sound stilted and unnatural. Use the discussion times—*(May respond)* in the youth parts—to probe your youth's understanding. Then share your own viewpoints, uncertainties, struggles, and faith. The more time you allow for spontaneous conversation, the more benefit you both will receive.

There are basic foundations to our understanding of the Bible. Yet theologians continue to disagree about some points. If you are uncomfortable with an idea presented, pray and reflect about it ahead of time. Give yourself the opportunity to discover new ways of understanding our God. If your discomfort remains, feel free to disagree and explain to your youths why.

Although the conversations appear to be written for one adult and one youth, likely you will have more than two people present. Pencil in names to divide the conversations, and involve everyone so that no one is left on the sidelines. This will help increase concentration levels.

For convenience, the conversations are divided into parts of similar lengths. How you handle the parts depends on the attention span of your youths. After the first conversation, you may decide to read the "Historical Peacemaker" story. After the second dialogue, you may read the printed interview with a "Contemporary Peacemaker" or offer a live interview with a peacemaker (see page 22). You might use all four parts on separate occasions. If you prefer to complete an entire session at once, be sensitive to how much your youths can absorb.

Each conversation includes a time of review, both at the beginning and the end. While this sounds monotonous, it does ingrain the concepts more firmly. Use these reviews as it suits your family and setting. You may choose to lighten this checkup by inventing a game you can play together.

Prayers

Why do we teach our youths to pray for peace? Henri Nouwen says,[1]

> Prayer—living in the presence of God—is the most radical peace action we can imagine. Prayer is peacemaking and not simply the preparation before, the support during, and the thanksgiving after. Prayer is not primarily a way to get something done. In prayer we undo the fear of death and therefore the basis of all human destruction.

Unless we are prepared and grounded in prayer and our relationship to God, our work for peace and justice is a futile attempt to save ourselves and our world. But when we learn to work side by side with God, continuing Jesus' mission with the guidance of the Holy Spirit, we act in response to the love we've been given. This love gives us courage to overcome our fears and take the seemingly ridiculous steps God asks of us.

The prayers included are simple and short. Don't limit yourselves to them! Before praying, take time to talk about the joys and concerns of your junior youths and include these. Also pray for missionaries and relief and development workers around the world as they help others make peace with God and neighbors. Contact your mission boards and relief agencies for prayer calendars. Be aware of violence in the world around you, and bring areas of conflict before God in your prayers.

Historical Peacemaker Stories

Those who make peace today point to stories they heard as children which inspired them. We often learn best through stories. Two which have had an especially impressive impact on Mennonites are Dirk Willems, who rescued his captor, and Preacher Peter, who had a thatched roof. Both are included in this book, along with four others.

But there are many more stories of courage available! Invest in several of the collections of stories suggested and make them available to your youths (see appendix 2). Read them aloud on family trips. These are the peace heroes your youths need for inspiration.

Contemporary Peacemaker Interviews

Peacemaking is alive and exciting today! Christians continue to take their stand for peace and justice in the face of violence. Take time to absorb and discuss a bit of the life of these special people. Each person interviewed responds to the same basic questions, in print, or orally if you recruit a local peace model. Mennonite Central Committee, your pastor, mission board, or church conference peace office can help you find a peacemaker willing to talk with your youth.

1. As you were growing up, what stories from Jesus' life and church history helped you decide to be a peacemaker?

2. What do you remember about being a peacemaker when you were a child?

3. How are you making peace now? What are you learning about God's way of peace?

Together reflect on things raised in the interview and dialogue with your local peacemaker.

Biblical Dramas

To involve the youths in the drama of the Bible, four short Bible scripts are included. Use them *before* the appropriate session readings as a *preview.* "Notes to Parents" will point out which scripts to use and when. These passages are perhaps less familiar, yet they are important to the understandings of peace. When possible, I've stayed close to the NRSV reading to help the youths realize that the Bible is not a dreary old book, but full of sparkling life and dark torment. The way was not always clear for those whose stories are recorded. They also had questions and many had to learn their lessons the hard way.

Projects

This list of ideas is included to aid your family as you further integrate peacemaking into your daily life (see appendix 3). Don't overly burden yourself! Projects shouldn't be drudgery, but rather an outgrowth of new understandings. Explain to your youths the reasons for the project, but don't lose heart if they don't completely understand. Later in life they will reevaluate experiences. Meanwhile, you are laying important foundation stones.

Session 6 includes time for you to introduce a family project, but you needn't wait until then! Look over the list early in the study. If your family has unexpected time to do something special, you'll already have ideas in mind.

Planning Time Together

The best setting for these sessions is an uninterrupted half-hour of parents and youths together. Turn off the stereo and TV and turn on the phone answering machine. Give your youths your undivided attention and thus let them know that this time together is valuable. By concentrating on your youths and their needs, you greatly increase your chances of capturing their enthusiasm. One family who gave the book a test run was amazed that their daughter actually begged for the sessions. She craved the intense time of their interaction.

If times like these cannot be a part of your family life, don't despair! Perhaps you can read through a session during a meal or immediately after school. Or save the book for a family trip, when you'll be on top of each other for hours on end. Some of the stories might be brief enough to read before the youths leave for school in the morning. Don't worry about setting aside several weeks and neatly completing the study. Complete what you can now and come back to the rest later. Something is better than nothing!

Other Uses for This Book

While this book was written for parents and junior youths, others can reap benefits from it. It could be used for:

1. *Mentor-youth study.* Many congregations now encourage mentor relationships between youth and adult (other than one of the parents) to support teens during difficult years. Because Bible study, discussion time, and chances to examine life choices are included, this book is excellent for these times together. For more information on mentoring, see *Side by Side*, by Lavon J. Welty (1989); and *One on One,* by Steve Roop (1993). (Both are from Newton, Kan.: Faith & Life Press; and Scottdale, Pa.: Mennonite Publishing House.)

2. *Sunday school or Bible school classes.* If your congregation hasn't used curriculum which emphasizes the peace stance recently, this book may fill that gap. For further help, see appendix 5. Teachers may choose to break up the readings even further and include hands-on projects to spice up each session.

3. *Sunday evening services.* If several groups in the congregation (families, classes, or mentor-youth pairs) are using the materials, a Sunday evening can be set aside to celebrate learnings. This special event would provide an incentive to complete the study in due time. All ages can join in acting out the Bible dramas and historic peacemaker stories as skits, possibly using costumes and props. Everyone can bring the products of their family projects and share banners, songs, responses to letters, and Peacebooks. Show videos from Mennonite Central Committee (MCC, Box 500, Akron, PA 17501-0500; or 134 Plaza Dr., Winnipeg, MB R3T 5K9). Serve cookies cut in the shape of doves and "peace punch" for refreshments. Some churches may choose to award prizes or certificates to those who have completed the study or who can say all the memory verses (include the adults!). Quizzes could be held over the concepts and Bible passages in the book.

4. *Small groups.* Families may choose to work together on the studies in small-group settings including junior youths. In this larger group, you may choose to shorten the sessions and increase the discussion time so youths can recount more of their own experiences. This will make the study more contemporary. Be sure to include lots of hands-on exercises to balance the head work (see appendix 3).

5. *Congregational gift to youths.* Some congregations give children their own Bible when they enter second grade. This study would be an appropriate gift from the congregation when youths enter fifth or sixth grade. By making a formal presentation, congregations emphasize the importance of the peace position.

6. *Grandparent commitment.* Grandparents may choose to make a gift to their grandchildren of both this book and their time to study it together. Grandparents can create special times to enhance relationships as they pass on their precious heritage.

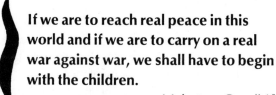

If we are to reach real peace in this world and if we are to carry on a real war against war, we shall have to begin with the children.

—*Mahatma Gandhi* [2]

Learning Goals

What do you hope to accomplish with your junior youths by using this book? What went through your mind when you decided to buy it? List at least three goals right here before continuing:

1.

2.

3.

4.

Did you include yourself and your relationship to your youths in any of the goals? If not, consider why this study might be important to you. Compose a goal about yourself:

As you look over the title and summary for each session, you will understand the goals set for the book. Other goals you might consider include (1) more complete Bible knowledge, (2) compassion for the enemy, (3) a better understanding of peace beliefs, and (4) a commitment to nonviolence.

How will you know if your goals have been accomplished? I will outline two basic ideas, but you will have more.

1. Before you begin the study, informally ask your youths about their viewpoints:

What is an enemy?

Why don't we go to war?

What is a peacemaker like? Do you know any?

Record their answers here or on another paper.

When you complete this study, ask your youths these same questions and record their answers here:

What growth do you find? What new understandings? What do you want to emphasize in future teaching? Record your thoughts here:

2. To evaluate how the study is going, think over these questions alone at the end of your times together:

a. Are your youths interested? Do they stop and ask questions about difficult concepts? Were they confused? Resistant to some ideas? Do they come back to the ideas later to continue struggling with them?

b. Were the setting and time good for your family? Helpful for the youths learning? Are there simple yet special things you can do to make the time more meaningful? (This might include lighting candles, gathering in a worshipful place, decorating with new peace posters [see appendix 2] and Bible verses, or following the time together with special foods.)

c. Can your youths make the jump from the biblical-theological materials to everyday applications? Do you see a change in attitudes? A new step on the journey?

d. What can you celebrate about your time together?

Can you affirm openness to new ideas? Delight in new insights? What have you learned from your youths?

e. Do some concepts need further work before you continue the study? Are there ideas in "Helps for Parents" which you can use? Can you ask your pastor or other friends to help you clarify your thoughts?

Co-Workers with God

As Paul points out in 1 Corinthians 3:8-9, we are only God's servants: "The one who plants and the one who waters have a common purpose, and each will receive wages according to the labor of each. For we are God's servants, working together; you are God's field, God's building."

While we are responsible for our own faith and growth, we are only indirectly responsible for that of our youths. We plant, the congregation waters, but God gives the growth. By *planting* I mean that we give our youths good soil to encourage them to put down firm roots. We are also careful not to hinder growth. But God is the one who gives the growth. Peace is the fruit of God's Spirit (Gal. 5:22).

As an uncertain young mother, I basked in the warmth of a comment from a parenting book, "You're a better parent than you think." While I tried to meet the needs of a demanding infant, balance household responsibilities, and sort between conflicting advice, I was relieved to know that *somebody* believed in me!

I would like to pass that affirmation on to you. Perhaps you are feeling overwhelmed with the responsibility of raising your youths to claim the peace heritage. Maybe other events have stretched the limits of your relationships, or your energy level is low and you feel inadequate.

Relax! *God is holding you!*

One of my favorite images of God is a needlepoint by Liz Wenger, "God So Loved the World." She represents God cra-

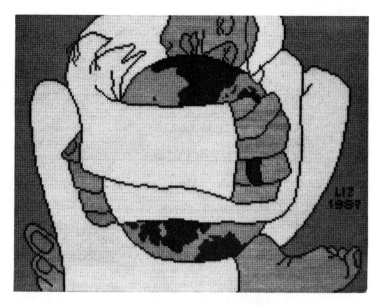

dling the world, with both arms and legs wrapped around protectively. God's expression is ecstasy mixed with delight.[3]

Here is Joe Hertzler's interpretation of the work:

> In warm embrace God cradles the world
>   like a child hugging a prized possession
>   like a mother cradling her child
>   like the father in Jesus' parable welcoming back
>   his lost son with a ring of acceptance
>   like the Creator who declares
>   "Behold, it is very good."

When you fear the adequacy of your parenting skills, the choices your youths make, or the minimal place God holds in your family life—remember, *God is holding you!*

This is the same God whose joyful voice rings out, "Fear not." May you go with God and God with you.

The Spirit of the Lord is
        upon me,
    because he has anointed me
    to bring good news
        to the poor.
He has sent me to proclaim
    release to the captives
    and recovery of sight
        to the blind,
    to let the oppressed go free,
    to proclaim the year of the
        Lord's favor.

Luke 4:18-19

Session 1

Jesus Came to Bring Peace

Summary: We don't go to war because we follow Jesus. Jesus came to bring peace and help others. If we want to follow Jesus, we will do the same.

Memory Verse: *Blessed are the peacemakers, for they will be called children of God* (Matthew 5:9).

Bible Texts Behind Session 1

Isaiah 61:1-2

Matthew 5:9

Matthew 5:38-39

Matthew 5:43-48

Matthew 6:25-34

Matthew 26:36-56

Luke 2:10-11,14

Luke 4:18-19, 25-27

Luke 23:34

John 6:1-15

John 12:12-19

John 19:20-23

PART A

Story: Jesus' birth was greeted by angels, who told the shepherds, "Do not be afraid. Jesus came to bring peace."

Faith Focus: Our fears cause us to be angry with others. Jesus helps us overcome these fears so we can love others. Peacemakers are like Jesus.

Notes to Parents

Before you begin, think about your answers to these questions:

1. What do you remember of your own and your family's experiences during the Persian Gulf War and any other wars you remember?

2. What fears lead you to hate or mistrust other people? What fears lead countries to go to war? How does Jesus help you deal with these fears?

3. Fear may seem like a strange place to begin this study. Pause a moment and consider: What stops you from making more peace in the world? Fear that you'll be misunderstood or ostracized? Fear that you'll lose financial security? Fear that God won't carry through on promises? Jim Wallis says, "We have allowed our faith and security in God to be overcome by fear, the greatest enemy of faith and its final contradiction."[1] Overcoming this fear is the most important place to start!

Youth-Adult Conversation

Adult: In early 1991, the United States was at war in the Persian Gulf. This may be the first war you've experienced. What do you remember about that war?

Youth: *(May respond.[2])*

Adult: *(Share your own memories.)* Today we begin, together, trying to understand why we don't go to war. During this war many parents realized that their youth didn't understand the church's peace position. Some families were confused about how to respond to a war which many others thought was good. What do you remember our family doing during the war?

Youth: *(May respond.)*

Adult: *(Add your own thoughts.)* Children and youths were confused. They didn't know what to do when schools told them to wear yellow ribbons and write letters to members of the military. What do you remember happening at your school?

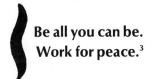

Youth: *(May respond.)*

Adult: How did you feel about all that happened?

Youth: *(May respond.)*

Adult: I want to spend time with you discussing the Bible, church history, and how we live.

Youth: Many of our friends at school who supported the war are Christians.

Adult: Even the president, who decided to go to war, says he is a Christian.

Youth: Why do we believe it is wrong to go to war? What is different about us?

Adult: We try to live like Jesus, the Prince of Peace. We take seriously the way Jesus lived and his call for us to live the same way.

Be all you can be.
Work for peace.[3]

Youth: Do you mean I should always wear sandals and let my hair grow like Jesus in some pictures?

Adult: To live like Jesus, we copy his relationship with God and how he treated people. We also think Jesus truly meant the things he said, and we try to follow those ideas in our lives.

Youth: What are Jesus' ideas?

Adult: Let's look at Jesus' life and teachings and see what he said about war and violence and peace.

Youth: Let's begin with Christmas! Is there anything about peace in that story?

Adult: Do you remember the first thing the angel told the shepherds? It's in Luke.

Youth: "Do not be afraid; for see—I am bringing you good news of great joy for all the people: to you is born this day in the city of David a Savior, who is the Messiah, the Lord" (Luke 2:10-11).

Adult: **Don't be afraid!** That's one of the first things angels tell humans when they visit them. It's an important first point. This was one reason Jesus came as a Savior to us all, to take away our fears.

Youth: What do you mean, take away our fears?

Adult: Jesus urges us to depend on God and not worry or fear so much (Matthew 6:25-34). Right now we are talking about fears because they sometimes lead us to be afraid of others, and then we hate them. *(Explain some of your own fears to the youths.)* What are your fears that cause you to be afraid of others?

Youth: *(May respond, for example, by naming fear that others will make fun of me.)*

Adult: Often it is our fears that lead us to war. Sometimes countries go to war because they are afraid of another country. One country might not want another to become too powerful. What are some other fears that cause nations to go to war?

Youth: *(May respond, for example, mentioning fear that another country will steal its land.)*

Adult: *(Add your own ideas.)* But Jesus loves us and helps us overcome our fears so we can love others.

Youth: This is a new thought for me. Fear stops us from making peace with others.

Adult: Fear is the opposite of faith. When we learn to love and depend on Jesus, he gives us strength so we can show love to those who hate us.

Youth: That's hard to do!

Adult: We'll talk some more about loving enemies in session 2. Look back at Luke 2:10-11 for an idea we'll talk about in session 5.

Youth: It says that this great joy is to be to *all* peoples.

Adult: We'll talk more about love for all peoples. What else did the angels say here in Luke?

Youth: "Glory to God in the highest heaven,
and on earth peace among those whom he favors" (Luke 2:14). Jesus is barely born, and angels are already talking about peace!

Adult: Right! The shepherds knew about the kind of peace the Roman government brought them. The mighty Roman army gave military security. The shepherds were safe from attacks from other countries.

Youth: But I don't think that's the kind of peace this is talking about.

Adult: I agree. The shepherds were poor, and they were interested in God's kind of peace.

Youth: What is God's peace?

Adult: We'll talk more about that in session 4. For now, let's say that to the poor, true peace includes having enough food, clothing, shelter, and God's gift of life. That is justice.

Youth: Why did the angels begin by saying,
"Glory to God in the highest heaven"?

Adult: The angels started by worshiping God, who alone is worthy to be worshiped. The Roman emperor also liked to be worshiped.

Youth: You mean the emperor, who was like our president, wanted people to worship him?

Adult: Yes. But the angels reminded the shepherds that we owe our obedience and worship first of all to God.

We'll talk about that more in session 3.

Youth: I see that when Jesus was born, the angels talked about peace. What did Jesus say about peace when he grew up?

Adult: Quite a bit! Next time we'll discuss that and why Jesus thought he came. Now let's review. What did we learn about Jesus and fear?

Youth: *(May respond.)*

Adult: Let's repeat the memory verse together.

All: **"Blessed are the peacemakers, for they will be called children of God"** (Matthew 5:9).

Adult: Let's close with prayer *(including joys and sorrows)*.

All: **"Almighty and loving God, who broke into the darkness of our world not with the cry of battle but with the cry of a baby, break into our lives this [evening]. Fill us with a vision of your peace on earth and good will among all people, so that even in the midst of brokenness and conflict we may have hope, through Jesus Christ our Lord. Amen."[4]**

Notes to Parents

1. How did this reading go? See the questions of point 2 under "Learning Goals" in the Introduction, "For Adults." How can you make your time together more effective? Encourage as much discussion as possible, and emphasize how beliefs influence the way we live.

2. In her book *Peacemaking: The Journey from Fear to Love*, Ronice E. Branding connects fear with our inability to act for peace.[5]

God's love is a source of strength. . . . It is the security of God's love that will enable us to move from fear and defensiveness to hope and vulnerability. For it is then that our perspective is changed and the questions are reframed. Instead of wondering "What difference can I

make?" and "How will I protect myself?" we begin to con-
sider "How am I to be faithful to God's will for justice?
What can I do to nurture compassion and reconciliation?
What can I risk to counteract violence?"

Consider what fears stop you from acting for peace. How
will you learn to trust God and overcome these fears?

3. As you are with your youths, take the opportunity to review these teachings on Jesus' birth and how fears lead us to
hate. Think together about the connections between fear and
hate as you read stories or watch TV together. Help your
youths learn to understand their own emotions better so they
can be more in control. Share with them your fears and hates,
how you work through these, and how your relationship with
Jesus has helped you.

PART B

Story: Some people expected Jesus to make war against the
Gentiles, like King David did. But Jesus lived as
apeacemaker, loving even his enemies.

Faith Focus: Jesus teaches us to love our enemies. As followers of Jesus, we look to him for help as we try to
love our enemies.

Notes to Parents

1. Each time you are together, begin with a review to reinforce learning.

2. Meditate for a few minutes on the contrast between the
way Jesus lived and the life of those taking part in war. Can the
true goals of God be accomplished through war?

3. Review this vocabulary with the youths.

Word List

Gentiles   The Jews were God's chosen people, the people of Israel. They called others Gentiles, the nations.

Messiah   The Old Testament foretold the coming of the Messiah-King, the Savior, to save God's people.

Palestine   Jesus and many of the Jews lived in Palestine, part of the world now called Israel and the West Bank.

Roman government   The Romans ruled the world when Jesus lived. The Jews hated them and wanted to rule their own country.

synagogue   Each Jewish community had its own synagogue, a house for prayer and worship.

Zealots   Jews who fought to overthrow the Romans.

Youth-Adult Conversation

Adult: Let's begin by reviewing what we talked about last time. What do you remember about the angels?

Youth: *(May respond.)*

Adult: Now we'll skip directly to what we think is the core of Jesus' teaching, the Sermon on the Mount.

Youth: The Sermon on the Mount? Why is it called that?

Adult: Jesus sat on a hillside while he taught so people could see him better and think of him as a new Moses. Our memory verse comes from this collection of Jesus' teachings. Let's repeat it together.

All: **"Blessed are the peacemakers,**
  for they will be called children of God"
   (Matthew 5:9).

Adult: Children are like their parents. What are some things the same about them?

Youth: *(May respond.)* Sometimes children and parents have eyes or noses that look alike. Sometimes they use their hands to make similar gestures.

Adult: Sometimes they are interested in the same hobbies or occupations. What are some things the same about you and me?

Youth: *(May respond.)*

Adult: In this passage, Jesus is saying that if you are a peacemaker, you are like God. There is a family resemblance[6] between God and those who make peace. God claims as children those working for peace.

Youth: But what did Jesus even know about war? No one asked him to be in the army! Some say that armies help keep the peace.

Adult: Jesus had a chance to be the leader of a Jewish army. Some of Jesus' friends wanted him to get rid of the Romans, who tortured some Jews. The Jews hated the Romans. But Jesus chose a different way.

Youth: I never knew that some of Jesus' friends wanted him to start an army!

Adult: Many Jews of Jesus' time thought the promised Messiah would be a conquering king, like the famous warrior King David.

Youth: So when Jesus came and started talking about being the Messiah from the Old Testament, they thought Jesus would be like David and chase the Romans away?

Adult: Right! These people wanted to kick the Roman enemy out of Palestine. They dreamed of a time when the Jewish people would have their own country again. These Jews were called Zealots.

Youth: Zealots? Did these people ever get rid of the Romans?

Adult: They tried. About 40 years after Jesus' death, they created a huge uprising, the Jewish War, which the Romans put down with much bloodshed.

Youth: Were any of Jesus' disciples Zealots?

Adult: Simon, one of Jesus' disciples, is called a Zealot. Some of Jesus' other disciples had ideas like the Zealots.

Youth: But where do you find verses in the Bible about people wanting Jesus to be a king?

Adult: Remember when Jesus fed the 5,000 (John 6:1-15)? At
that time the people intended to make him a king, to
create a kingdom of *this* world with Jesus as the leader. But Jesus slipped away quietly.

Youth: That's one. Is there another?

Adult: A different time masses of people sang praises to Jesus
and called him their king, making the Pharisees furi-
ous (John 12:12-19). Do you remember that story?

Youth: You mean on Palm Sunday, when Jesus rode a donkey?

Adult: Right! Can you imagine what a strange sight that
must have been: a crowd of people praising Jesus, who
rode a lowly donkey as a king!

Youth: In that time, how did other kings travel?

Adult: They rode in chariots with fast horses so they could
move quickly in battle. Jesus had different ideas about
what kind of kingdom he was bringing. He wouldn't
be a warrior-leader driving a chariot to make war
against the Romans.

Youth: I've never heard of a donkey leading an army to war!
Jesus must have come for a different reason than to
make war.

Adult: Good point! Let's look at Luke to discover what Jesus
saw as his God-given task. One Sabbath, Jesus was visiting in his hometown, Nazareth. He was invited to
read Scripture at the synagogue. This is what he read.

Youth: "The Spirit of the Lord is upon me,
     because he has anointed me to bring
         good news to the poor.
He has sent me to proclaim release to the captives
     and recovery of sight to the blind,
         to let the oppressed go free,
         to proclaim the year of the Lord's favor"
             (Luke 4:18-19).

Adult: Do you understand this? What does it mean "to let the
oppressed go free"? To "bring good news to the poor"?

Youth: *(May respond.)*

Adult: *(Answer any questions.)* Jesus was quoting from Isaiah 61:1-2. But the people became angry! He stopped reading too soon. He left out the last part of verse two, the part about God pouring vengeance on Gentiles. This part was special to his listeners. Can you explain the word *vengeance?*

Youth: *(May respond.)*

Adult: The Jews wanted God to take their side, to get even for them for all they had suffered. They hoped he would take bloody revenge on the Gentiles, especially the hated Romans.

Youth: But Jesus didn't go on and talk about punishing the Gentiles.

Adult: Correct. When we read further in Luke, we see that he talked about times when God *favored* Gentiles instead of Jews (Luke 4:25-27). Jesus spoke words of grace, explaining that he came to save everyone, including the Jews' enemies.

Youth: I'll bet that made the Jews angry!

Adult: Right! The crowd got so mad that they hustled him out to throw him off a cliff. But again, he walked away!

Youth: And what does this have to do with not going to war?

Adult: What do you think?

Youth: (May respond.)
Adult: The Jews wanted God and Jesus to make war against the Gentiles. Instead, Jesus explained that he came to love the Gentiles as well as the Jews.
Youth: So Jesus' mission, and the mission of those who follow him, is not to make war against enemies, but to show God's love to enemies.
Adult: Since Jesus and his life are central to our understanding of peace, we'll spend more time looking at his life next time. Let's pray.
All: **"O Lord, open my eyes**
that I may see the need of others,
Open my ears that I may hear their cries,
Open my heart so that they need not be without succor.
Let me not be afraid to defend the weak
because of the anger of the strong,
nor to defend the poor
because of the rich.
Show me where love and hope and faith are needed,
and use me to bring them to these places.
Open my eyes and ears that I may, this coming day,
be able to do some work of peace for [you. Amen.]" [7]

PART C

Story: Jesus decided not to strike back or to hurt those who hurt him.

Faith Focus: Jesus encourages us to stop violence by surprising others with God's love.

Notes to Parents
1. *Nonresistance* is a core Mennonite belief, but the term

may be unfamiliar to others. According to a Mennonite Confession of Faith, it "describes the way in which Jesus endured accusation and abuse, yet did not strike back violently. Instead, he entrusted himself to God's ultimate justice. The same nonresistant way is commended to his disciples (1 Peter 2:21-24)."[8] Acting to break the cycle of violence is another way to describe nonresistance.

2. For those of us not familiar with Middle Eastern fighting techniques, here is some background to Matthew 5:38-39. When someone uses a right hand to strike another on the right cheek, this likely is an insult rather than the beginning of a fistfight. It is a backhanded slap. By calmly turning the left cheek, one is refusing to be insulted, asking instead to be treated as an equal, someone worthy of being slapped by the open palm!

3. In the past, this stand was too often misunderstood to mean that those being abused or mistreated should not seek justice. A better interpretation is that followers of Jesus should nonviolently confront offenders with the effects of their behavior and try to overcome evil with good.[9]

Word List
nonresistance   Showing God's love and peace by refusing to hurt those who hurt you.

Youth-Adult Conversation

Youth: Last time we talked about showing God's love to enemies. When someone is mean to us, how do we show love? It doesn't sound natural.

Adult: It's not natural at all. Jesus gives us some ideas in Matthew.

Youth: "You have heard that it was said, 'An eye for an eye and a tooth for a tooth.' But I say to you, Do not resist an evildoer. But if anyone strikes you on the right cheek, turn the other also" (Matthew 5:38-39).

An eye for an eye and a tooth for a tooth—that way everyone in the world will soon be blind and toothless.

—*Fiddler on the Roof* [10]

Adult: Jesus begins with what seems natural. The old way was, if someone knocks out your tooth, you get to knock out one of theirs.

Youth: Like when I was a child and someone hit me, I thought it was fair to hit back.

Adult: But Jesus says not to hit back. Then he gives surprising ideas about what to do next.

Youth: So Jesus tells me to let someone who has slapped me on one cheek slap the other also. What kind of sense does that make? That's *opposite* from what I want to do!

Adult: His ideas do make us wonder. How would you describe a fight?

Youth: Well, if someone hits me, I'll probably hit them back a little harder. Then they'll think they have the right to kick me, and I'll kick back rougher, and on and on. I guess Jesus' way stops the fight from getting worse.

Adult: We call Jesus' way of stopping the violence *nonresistance.*

Youth: Do you mean, don't resist by hurting others?

Adult: Yes. But it's more than not hitting back. It's surprising the other with God's love. This breaks the cycle of violence.

Youth: It also shows the other a bit about what Jesus is like.

Jesus made a decision not to hurt those who tried to destroy him.

Adult: The Spirit gave Jesus strength not to hurt those who hurt him. That same Spirit is ours and ready to help us love enemies and surprise them with God's love and peace. When did Jesus decide not to hurt those who hurt him?

Youth: *(May respond.)* I especially remember that eventful evening in the Garden of Gethsemane (Matthew 26:36-56).

Adult: Right. Jesus was facing arrest and almost certain death at the hands of his enemies. Surely, his disciples thought, at such an important moment, it was okay to use violence.

Youth: That's when one took out a sword and cut off the high priest's servant's ear. But then Jesus healed the ear!

Adult: I wish I could have seen that. Do you think he just said "poof!" and put the ear back on?

Youth: Maybe. But it reminds me of what we were just talking about. Jesus came to heal, not to hurt. He didn't even defend himself before the high priest, when he was hit or whipped or nailed to the cross.

Adult: Those verses, and the whole life of Jesus, ask us to feed the hungry, give drink to the thirsty, clothe the naked, welcome the homeless, visit the prisoner, and live God's peace and justice.

Youth: This is all starting to fit together! As followers of Jesus, we are to be like him, to imitate his life. But war does just the opposite. It makes others hungry, thirsty, homeless, prisoners, sick, and dead.[11]

Adult: When we make war, we go against all that Jesus taught, what Jesus claimed as his mission. Jesus wants us to love our enemies.

Youth: That's from Matthew. "You have heard that it was said, 'You shall love your neighbor and hate your enemy.' But I say to you, Love your enemies and pray for those who persecute you, so that you may be children of your Father in heaven;

Adult: "for he makes his sun rise on the evil and on the good, and sends rain on the righteous and on the un-righteous. For if you love those who love you, what reward do you have? Do not even the tax collectors do the same?

Youth: "And if you greet only your brothers and sisters, what more are you doing than others? Do not even the Gentiles do the same? Be perfect, therefore, as your heavenly Father is perfect" (Matthew 5:43-48). But I can't be perfect! That's just not possible!

Adult: Of course not. We're human and we make mistakes, especially if we try to live on our own. The joy and the wonder is that we are not alone. Other Christians can help us. What all-surpassing power helps us?

Youth: Jesus! The love Jesus showed us can help me to love my enemies.

Adult: Right! We often forget that Jesus is to be our model in all of life. God wants us to be followers of Jesus. Just as God gave Jesus strength to love his enemies—and even forgive them—so God will give strength to Jesus' followers.[12]

> **Love, as revealed and interpreted in the life and death of Jesus Christ, involves more than we have yet seen, and is the only power by which evil can be overthrown and the only sufficient basis for human society.**
>
> *—International Fellowship of Reconciliation[13]*

Youth: Jesus even forgave the people who hung him on the cross (Luke 23:34).

Adult: Since we started with the beginning of Jesus' life, let's finish with some of his last words to the disciples. After Jesus was raised, he went to the upper room to meet with the disciples who had betrayed him and left him alone to die (John 20:19-23). The first thing he said was, "Peace be with you." He showed them his hands and side, and then repeated

Youth: "Peace be with you." I like that. Jesus' life began and ended with peace.

Adult: So what is the first reason we don't go to war?

Youth: *(May respond.)*

Adult: Let's end by praying together.

All: **Lord Jesus, you were able to forgive and love those who hung you on the cross. We also thank you for forgiving us. Please help us learn to love our enemies and stop violence as you did. Guide our feet in your path of peace. Amen.**

Notes to Parents

1. If this study has piqued your interest in rereading Jesus' life, choose Luke. Pay special attention to Jesus' conflicts with authority, which come through so well in Luke.

2. It is of vital importance that our children and youths experience forgiveness in the home. Children often mold their first image of God to resemble their parents. By dealing compassionately with our children's mistakes, we teach them that God also will forgive. Children who have experienced forgiveness are more willing to try risky things, like making peace.

Historic Peacemaker

At different times over the years since Jesus died, Christians have stopped and looked more carefully at the Bible. Often, at these points of renewal, they have chosen to follow Jesus by loving their enemies and not taking part in war. The Mennonites have come from one of these movements, called the Anabaptists. In 1539 Menno Simons, for whom these believers are named, wrote the following words:[14]

> **The regenerated do not go to war,**
> **nor engage in strife.**
> **They are the children of peace**
> **who have beaten their swords into plowshares**
> **and their spears into pruning hooks,**
> **and know of no war. . . .**
> **Since we are to be conformed**
> **to the image of Christ,**
> **how can we then fight our enemies**
> **with the sword? . . .**
> **Spears and swords of iron**
> **we leave to those who, alas,**
> **consider human blood and swine's blood**
> **of well-nigh equal value.**

Discussion Questions

Some of this may be hard to understand. Take a few moments to be sure all the ideas are clear.

1. Who are the *regenerated?*

2. What does it mean to "be conformed to the image of Christ"?

3. What does Menno Simons mean by comparing human blood and swine's blood?

❧   ❧   ❧

Following the Prince of Peace

Cornelia Lehn[15]

Menno Simons, a Catholic priest in Holland in the 1530s, was afraid. He sat reading in his church office. Studying the Bible had given him new ideas about how to live like Jesus.

"To follow in the footsteps of the Prince of Peace, who shed his blood for all of us alike, we must do *good* to those that hate us," he said aloud to himself. "We cannot kill them. Jesus said, 'The one who takes up the sword, shall perish by the sword.' That is as true now as it was then." Menno knew that Jesus taught against violence.

But many other people did not know what the Bible said. Others joined Menno in his new faith, but some of them also followed Jan van Leyden. Jan taught that they should form an army to help God.

And I am afraid to tell them they are wrong, thought Menno. I am afraid to teach them the way of the Lord, even though I know it. I am afraid of persecution. I am afraid to suffer with my Lord.

Some of Menno's new ideas about how to live were against the law. Those like him believed only adults should be baptized, and they were often captured and put to death. Sometimes they were cruelly tortured before they were killed.

Jan van Leyden decided to take over the city of Münster. He and his followers wanted to establish the New Jerusalem,

"God's holy city." They thought they could use military might to help God.

But Menno knew they were wrong. He told himself, "Christ did not bring in his kingdom with military might. He brought in his kingdom on the cross. And he did so when he could have called on more than twelve legions of angels to defend him. Christ would not allow Peter to defend him with the sword. How can Christians then defend themselves with it?"

Finally a friend came to Menno and begged him to write down how Jan van Leyden was wrong. "How can we sort all this out when we don't know the Scriptures?" he pleaded. "It is so hard when more and more of our loved ones are dying a martyr's death. It seems good and right to save them from torture by fighting back. Deep down, I know that is not the way to bring in Christ's kingdom. Menno, write a pamphlet describing your views so we can pass it around for people to read."

Menno took a deep breath. "Yes," he agreed. "I will start writing immediately."

So Menno wrote a booklet explaining his ideas against Christians using military might. He challenged Jan van Leyden and his teaching. But before it was even published, the government killed Jan and his followers in Münster, along with some persons from Menno's congregation and even Peter Simons, perhaps Menno's brother.

Now Menno could no longer be silent. He preached from the Bible openly and talked freely to individual people, even though he knew it was dangerous. He could no longer believe what the Bible said and then act as if he knew nothing about it. He felt responsible for the people who had new faith in Jesus Christ but who had no leader, like sheep without a shepherd. Menno was no longer afraid.

He spoke openly as long as he could, but early in 1536 it became clear that he would be arrested if he stayed in his congregation. One night he quietly slipped away. Menno gave up his good job and salary, his comfortable home and friends.

He was ready to follow wherever Christ would lead him.

After he was married, his wife, Gertrude, and their small children often traveled with him. Sometimes they had to go into hiding to escape the authorities. Later he wrote that in all the country, he could not find a "cabin or hut" where his "poor wife" and their children could stay in safety for a year or two.[16]

Thus Christ sent Menno Simons, a fugitive, out to gather the many people hungry for the Word of God. Menno preached, he taught, he counseled. Now the community of believers could together follow the Prince of Peace.

Contemporary Peacemaker

Menno Simons led the Mennonite church hundreds of years ago. Today Christian Peacemaker Teams (CPT) lead Mennonite and Church of the Brethren believers in making peace. Gene Stoltzfus works with this group. In this photo he is wearing a barrette for peace at the U.S. Embassy in Haiti. Read this interview with Gene, and/or interview a local peacemaker (see questions on page 22):

As I was growing up, the story from Jesus' life that perplexed me was the cleansing of the temple, because of the tough way Jesus dealt with the situation. The story of the Good Samaritan also affected me. The Samaritan combined compassion, charity, *and* firmness; he helped deliberately and at risk to himself. In my home we were encouraged to read *Martyrs Mirror* (available in your church library or from Herald Press), stories about Christians willing to die for their faith. The idea of people living out their convictions and being prepared to die was important to me as I was growing up.

In second or third grade, I was once tackled by some big high school boys in the washroom at school. They pushed me into a corner and started hollering at me because my people (my church) didn't go to war and that was bad. They were going to beat me up. So I didn't finish my work in the washroom. I got out of there as fast as I could. That was a major incident for me. I was really scared of those guys.

When I was in fifth or sixth grade, my parents were robbed and called the police. My brother came home and challenged my parents about calling the police. I was confused by that, but I learned about the problem of using force in the world.

Christian Peacemaker Teams try to organize the convictions, skills, and energy of children, youths, young adults, and adults of the Mennonites and Church of the Brethren. Each CPT trains them to do specific acts of peacemaking and doing justice. If they choose to take part, they benefit. There is far more ability, skill, and potential for peacemaking in our churches than has ever been mobilized.

Mystery surrounds undertaking a witness for peace. We sow a seed and don't know what the plant is going to look like. But it's planted, and the harvest will come, even though most people don't even know the seed has been sown. I've often seen breakthroughs in discussions and confrontations.

I look back on the peacemaking work in Vietnam. In 1963 I went and was there for five years. The war wasn't over until 1975, twelve long years. Sometimes I felt this thing would never end, that it would drag on and on and on. But that's not true! Our efforts don't change things immediately, but they do change the spiritual reality of what is around. They make it possible for people to think new thoughts, and they create a different culture and perception. I really believe that.

Christian Peacemaker Teams is here to help you and your congregation make peace and do justice. During Advent we help families including grandparents prepare for the nonviolent coming of Christ with actions against violent toys. For more information, contact me at Christian Peacemaker Teams, 1821 W. Cullerton, Chicago, IL 60608; phone 312 455-1199.

You have heard that it was said,
'You shall love your neighbor
and hate your enemy.'
But I say to you, Love your
enemies and pray for those
who persecute you, so that you
may be children of your Father
in heaven.

Matthew 5:43-45a

Session 2

God's Children Love Enemies

Summary: We don't go to war because Jesus taught us to love. When we love our enemies, we are sharing God's love and are known as God's children.

Memory Verse: *You have heard that it was said, 'You shall love your neighbor and hate your enemy.' But I say to you, Love your enemies and pray for those who persecute you, so that you may be children of your Father in heaven* (Matthew 5:43-45a).

Bible Texts Behind Session 2

Genesis 13, 14, 18	John 13:34-35
Genesis 26:12-22	Acts 7:54-60
Genesis 37, 42–46	Acts 16:1-34
Matthew 5:43-48	1 John 4:7-12
Luke 10:25-37	

PART A

Story: Many of God's people in the Old Testament practiced love of enemies.

Faith Focus: It takes extra effort to love enemies, but God gives us strength.

Notes to Parents

1. What points do you remember from session 1? What difference have the teachings from that lesson made in the way you have lived?

2. Can you remember when you loved an enemy? Do your youths know someone else who loved an enemy? Have your youths ever shown love for an enemy?

3. If some of these stories from Genesis (listed under Bible Texts) are unfamiliar to your youths, take the time to read them together. *Before* this session, read the biblical drama "Elisha Makes Peace" (see Contents for "Biblical Dramas").

Youth-Adult Reading

Adult: Last time we reviewed Jesus' life to see that he calls us to love, not to make war. What other things do you remember?

Youth: *(May respond.)*

Adult: We talked about many difficult issues that will take us a lifetime to sort out in the ways we live. *(Mention a teaching from last session and how it has affected the way you live.)*

Youth: *(May respond, or ask further questions.)*

Adult: We will continue, in the next times we have together, to discuss many of these ideas. This session we especially want to talk about how Jesus taught us to treat our enemies. Let's repeat our memory verse.

All: **"You have heard that it was said, 'You shall love your neighbor and hate your enemy.' But I say to you, Love your enemies and pray for those who persecute you, so that you may be children of your Father in heaven"** (Matthew 5:43-45a).

Youth: More talk about being the children of God!

Adult: Loving enemies and making peace are important characteristics of God.

> **Love is the most durable power in the world. . . . Love is the only force capable of transforming an enemy into a friend.**
>
> —*Martin Luther King, Jr.*[1]

Youth: I know that's what Jesus said, and last session made me realize that's what Jesus did. But it's really hard to love enemies!

Adult: I agree! There have been times in my life when I longed for revenge. When someone is mean to me, I find it almost impossible to love my enemies. *(Talk about such a time, if you can in a helpful, not hostile way.)*

Youth: *(May also talk about an enemy.)*

Adult: I'm only human, just like you, and just like many of the people in the Bible. Can you think of times in the Bible when someone had to try hard to love an enemy?

Youth: Well, the one I've heard over and over is the good Samaritan story (Luke 10:25-37).

Adult: That's a good place to start.

Youth: But those were national enemies! That Samaritan wasn't being kind to someone who had hurt him *personally.*

Adult: You're right. But if we think together, we can find stories of folks who forgave others who were really mean to them personally. Let's look in the Old Testament. Start with Joseph and his brothers, who sold him to slavery in Egypt.

Youth: Well, you're correct that Joseph didn't kill his brothers or let them starve to death, but he certainly enjoyed making them sweat for a while! (Genesis 37, 42–46).

Adult: Joseph wanted to test his brothers, to see if they had changed. But they did have a joyful reunion at last. Whom else do you remember?

Youth: Abram decided it was better to divide land between him and Lot rather than have their servants fighting over it. He even let Lot have the well-watered land (Genesis 13).

Adult: Soon after that, when Lot was taken captive, Abram rescued him, even though he could have been angry that Lot took the better land (Genesis 14). Later, Abraham pleaded with God to save Sodom and, at the same time, Lot (Genesis 18).

Youth: Isaac preferred to move away rather than quarrel over wells (Genesis 26:12-22).

Adult: In a desert land where water was difficult to find, Isaac must have been very committed to peace. It took extra effort to move when the herdsmen of Gerar were being so unfair.

Youth: Extra effort! Loving enemies is so hard. Where do we get that extra effort?

Adult: I think it comes from our relationship with God. God made promises to Abraham, and he believed God would keep those promises.

**The ultimate miracle of love is this . . .
that love is given to us to give to one
another.**

—Anonymous[2]

Youth: But how do promises help us love enemies?

Adult: When people believe in God's promises, that is called
faith. When we have faith in God, we believe God did
the impossible before and will do it again.

Youth: And loving enemies *is* the impossible!

Adult: Joseph, Abraham, and Isaac all had close relationships
with God. They believed God's promises. When they
relied on God, God gave them strength.

Youth: And this strength helped them love their enemies?

Adult: Yes. And that same strength will help us love our enemies. It isn't easy.

Youth: But I have the promise that God will help me.

Adult: Let's pray about that.

All: **Lord, you kept your promises to Abraham, Isaac, and
Joseph. Please also keep your promises to us. Help us
to love our enemies, especially when that seems impossible. Guide our feet in your path to peace. Amen.**

Notes to Parents

1. Do your youths understand what an enemy is? Can they
name some? Can you name your own? These passages don't
say *not* to have enemies—we all have them, even if only
through their choice. But God guides us in how to treat these
enemies and try to turn them into friends.

2. How do you help your youths come into a relationship
with God from which they can draw strength? One way is to be
willing to share how you depend on God. Can you think of others?

PART B

Story: Stephen, Paul and Silas showed love to their enemies.

Faith Focus: When we show love to our enemies, they see God's love in us.

Notes to Parents

If your youths haven't recently studied the stoning of Stephen (Acts 6:8—8:1) or the adventure Paul and Silas had in jail (Acts 16:1-34), you might want to review the stories together before you begin.

Loving enemies demands creativity and the Spirit of God dwelling within us. Morton Kelsey, in *Caring*[3] points out that we can't claim to love those we don't like.

> Let me say very clearly and simply that loving without liking is not loving at all. Please deliver me from the love of people who do not like me. Genuine love is a quality of caring which finds something appealing in the other person as well as making the heroic effort to "love." We are beginning to follow the way of love, the way of Christ, when our loving and our liking begin to converge. This does not imply that we approve of everything that other people are doing, for they may be causing harm and hurt. But we can still care for them and love them.

While there is no formula for loving enemies which always works, Kelsey claims the following steps help when he "puts [his] energy into working at them."

1. Realize we have enemies. These are people who do not like us as well as people we do not like. Admit how little we know about how to love even our family and friends and even less about loving enemies (Matthew 5:21-26).

2. Stop doing anything unkind to the enemy. Learn to handle anger constructively. To control anger:

a. Write it down and look at it in black and white.

b. Talk it over with a friend.

c. Look for the cause of the anger, and change what is upsetting you.

d. If you can't change the cause, cry out to God, who understands your agony and can comfort you (Matthew 5:38-42).

3. Don't gossip. Negative criticism has nothing to do with love (Exodus 20:16).

4. Pray for your enemy. One concrete way is to pray the Lord's Prayer for them (Matthew 5:44).

5. Find something positive about your enemy, and tell someone else about it.

6. Perform a kind act for your enemy. It is nearly impossible to dislike someone you've made happy!

Children should be reminded, however, that they are not expected to face these issues alone. Let them know that they can and should ask an adult for help if they are being mistreated or abused.

Youth-Adult Conversation

Adult: Last time we talked about people from the Old Testament who loved their enemies. We included Joseph, Abraham, and Isaac. *(Name your favorite, and explain why.)* Who was your favorite?

Youth: *(May respond.)*

Adult: We also talked about the strength God gives us by keeping promises.

Youth: I understand that God keeps the promise of helping us to love enemies, but it still sounds difficult.

Adult: And it is! But as we examine more stories, we may find more ways to love enemies. In the New Testament, who showed love to enemies?

Youth: *(May respond.)* Stephen reminds me a lot of Jesus, dying while saying, "Lord, do not hold this sin against them" (Acts 7:54-60).

Adult: Just before he was stoned, Stephen looked up to heaven and saw Jesus. That must have given him strength as he was being killed. Whom else do you remember?

Youth: Paul and Silas stopped the jailkeeper from harming himself when they could have escaped from jail (Acts 16:1-34).

Adult: And that very night, the jailkeeper and his whole family were baptized.

Youth: You know, if Paul had been sitting in jail that night, angrily stewing about how the jailer mistreated him, that jailer would have been dead, rather than a new believer in Jesus.

Adult: Keep going. What might that mean about loving enemies?

Youth: Perhaps, when we are seeking revenge against someone, we are keeping them from the chance of knowing Jesus.

Adult: Or at least from the opportunity of seeing Jesus' love in our lives.

Youth: Remember the song, "They'll Know We Are Christians by Our Love"?

Adult: That is based on what Jesus said in John. Let's read those verses.

Youth: "I give you a new commandment, that you love one another. Just as I have loved you, you also should love one another. By this everyone will know that you are

All works of love are works of peace.
                                              —Mother Teresa[4]

my disciples, if you have love for one another" (John 13:34-35).

Adult: First John also tells us that our love for each other reflects the love of God.

Youth: In this is love, not that we loved God but that he loved us and sent his Son to be the atoning sacrifice for our sins. "Beloved, since God loved us so much, we also ought to love one another." (1 John 4:10-11).

Adult: Jesus asks us to show love to our enemies so they would come to know the love of God through our family resemblance. They will experience God's love through us. Let's repeat our memory verse.

All: **"You have heard that it was said, 'You shall love your neighbor and hate your enemy.' But I say to you, Love your enemies and pray for those who persecute you, so that you may be children of your Father in heaven"** (Matthew 5:43-45a).

Adult: How can we love our enemies?

Youth: *(May respond.)*

Adult: Love is more than a feeling. It's the way we act, the things we do for another person.

Youth: As when Paul and Silas stopped the jailkeeper from killing himself?

Adult: Right! Loving enemies means praying for them and hoping good things happen in their lives.

Youth: And then helping those good things to happen?

Adult: You're catching on.

Youth: But that still doesn't make it easy!

Adult: You're right. But Jesus nowhere promised that it would be easy, only that he would be with us.

Youth: Some of the people we talked about were very brave to keep loving. I guess they are heroes of love!

Adult: I like that. When it is difficult for us to love our enemies, we can learn to be brave with God's love and help from other Christians. Because we ourselves

Youth: So, when it's really hard to love someone who is mean to me, I should look to Jesus and the church for help.

Adult: That's right. You can pray and you can ask others for help. Then you'll be a hero of love! Now, what's the second reason we don't go to war?

Youth: *(May respond.)*

Adult: Let's pray.

All: **Lord God, who created us and all other peoples,**
Whose Son died and was raised to save everyone
from sin,
And whose Spirit lives among all humanity,
Teach us to love those we call enemy,
And give us the courage to do what seems impossible.
Help us to rely on your love when ours is weak
And your forgiveness when we fail.
In the name of the all-powerful, all-loving, and all-
forgiving God, Amen.

Notes to Parents

1. Paul watched Stephen being killed. Discuss with your youths how this might have influenced his life later on. How did Stephen help Paul understand that love is a part of God's character?

2. How do your youths experience the love of God? From you and your spouse? Your congregation? Can you talk together about times you've experienced God's love?

3. Who are your heroes of love? Can you tell their stories to your youths? Especially try to talk about people your family knows and simple events. Your youths will probably not experience an earthquake in jail soon, but they will deal with others who are mean.

Historic Peacemaker

Martyrs Mirror is a book which for centuries has shaped Mennonites and their belief in suffering rather than seeking revenge (available in your church library or from Herald Press). The stories, collected by Thieleman Jansz van Braght and published in Dutch in Holland in 1660, trace the ideas of believers baptism and nonresistance from the earliest days of Christianity. He hoped readers would be inspired to follow the faithfulness of those willing to die for their beliefs.

For the second edition, published in 1685, Jan Luyken engraved pictures to accompany many of the stories. The following engraving continues to be one of the first images called to mind by Mennonites who have chosen to love their enemies. The story is reprinted from *On Fire for Christ*, a recent imaginative retelling of fifteen stories from *Martyrs Mirror*, by Dave and Neta Jackson.

❧ ❧ ❧

1
Between Ice and Fire
Dirk Willems
(Asperen, Netherlands: 1569)

Dave and Neta Jackson[5]

The thiefcatcher pushed back his stool and stood up. He wasn't a tall man, but had a thick neck and broad shoulders and his presence seemed to fill the room. He eyed the burgomaster a moment, then growled, "Don't worry, chief. I'll have this Willems in the bag for you within the week."

The chief magistrate of Asperen laughed aloud. "I know, I know! That's why I hired you. 'Hartog always gets his man,' they say." The smile faded and the burgomaster suddenly jabbed his finger at the man across the desk. "Mind you," he scowled, "this Dirk Willems has given us the slip before. Don't let it happen this time. Swear to me!"

The thiefcatcher looked offended. "I told you. He'll be in your hands within the week."

"Swear on your honor!"

"I swear." Without another word Hartog stalked out the door.

That evening, the thiefcatcher took up a position in the shadows of a small street giving him a good view of the building opposite, a small shop with an outside stairway leading to the second story. He shivered as the cold penetrated his heavy coat. From time to time he blew on his hands, then shoved them back in his pockets, never taking his gaze from the stairs.

About nine o'clock a man and a woman came down the cobblestone street and went up the stairs. Hartog stared intently. The man could be Willems, he concluded—bearded chin, slight. . . . He fit the burgomaster's description. A light was struck and glowed softly from the upstairs window. The man in the shadows watched it, his mind racing. How best to get his man? He hadn't yet formed a plan. He had to be sure. He would come back before sunrise and track Willems' comings and goings. Then he'd know where and when to make his move. He needed some backup, too, in case Willems gave him any trouble. The burgomaster didn't tell him what they wanted him for, but he might be dangerous.

Satisfied with his initial stakeout, Hartog's thoughts turned to getting in from the cold night air. Starting out of the shadows, he suddenly saw another figure coming down the street. The thiefcatcher drew back. The figure stopped and held still as if listening. Hartog pressed his back against the cold stone. After a few moments, the figure—a man—ascended the stairs, knocked softly, then disappeared inside.

The thiefcatcher cursed under his breath. Had the man

seen him? He thought not. But he had to be more careful. He couldn't risk alerting his prey.

Several hours later, after some drinks and a nod in front of the fire at a local alehouse, Hartog slipped back to his observation point in the narrow street. The sun was not up yet, but the sky was turning a thin yellow. Everything was still in the building across the street.

A movement at the end of the street caught Hartog's eye. He squinted his eyes against the morning light and saw a man disappearing around the corner. Willems? He wasn't sure, but from this distance it could be. . . . But how did he get out of the building? With no more than a split-second hesitation, Hartog sprinted out of his hiding place and ran down the street. Rounding the corner, he saw the figure hurrying ahead of him, casting glances back over his shoulder.

It was Willems! In a hurry, too. Was he trying to give him the slip? The thiefcatcher acted on instinct, knowing the ways of men who are trying not to be caught. Keeping to shadows and doorways, he followed the figure, who kept up a snappy pace. A few more turns and streets and Hartog was sure. Willems was heading for the edge of town.

He was going to need help. Casting about among the few early passersby beginning to fill the streets, he saw one of the sheriff's men making his rounds. Taking a few precious seconds, he whispered urgently to the man, who then hurried back into town.

The sun was up as both prey and pursuer headed into the open fields. There was no slinking about here. Now Willems knew he was being followed. The man ahead began to run. The thiefcatcher picked up his pace. Where were his reinforcements? He couldn't keep this up much longer. His skills lay in stealth and surprise, not in running contests. Willems was older than he, but light and quick.

Willems left the road and started out over the winter stubble. He stumbled once and almost fell. Hartog hoped he was getting tired. The thiefcatcher caught a second wind and willed his legs faster.

Then ahead he saw the Linge, one of many small streams crisscrossing through the countryside, frozen by the long weeks of winter. He saw Willems hesitate, then step cautiously onto the ice. The man glanced over his shoulder at the thiefcatcher gaining on him rapidly and made his decision. Slipping badly, he scurried across the ice.

Hartog looked dubiously at the ice, but realized he had only one choice. The burgomaster would have his neck if he let this fish get away. He stepped out onto the ice. Willems was almost to the other side. Throwing caution to the wind, Hartog began to run.

The next moment he heard a sharp cracking sound, and suddenly cold black water closed over his head. He struggled to the top, grasping frantically for something solid. "Help!" he gasped. "Help me!" His arms found the jagged edge of ice, but

when he tried to pull himself out, it broke away and plunged him once more under the black water.

The next time his head broke out of the water, he heard a calm voice say, "Don't panic, man. Grab hold! Grab hold!" Peering through wet hair plastered against his eyes, he saw Willems lying on the ice, his coat flung ahead of him, a sleeve dragging in the water. Hartog grabbed and held. "Good, good," said the man above him. "Don't fight. Just hang on."

On the shore behind the thiefcatcher, a knot of people were gathering, yelling and shouting. Ignoring them, Willems inched away from the jagged hole. Hanging on to the coat, the thiefcatcher was pulled out of the water onto the ice. He lay there gasping, trying to catch his breath. Then he felt Willems tugging him further.

"Come on, man, we've got to get off the ice."

The pair stumbled on to dry ground. The thiefcatcher took a deep breath, turned and looked back to the other shore into the leering face of the burgomaster.

"Ha, ha, Hartog!" he called, laughing. "Did you get your man? Or did your man get you?"

The thiefcatcher looked at Willems, standing beside him. Willems returned his gaze, his eyes steady. Hartog turned back to the burgomaster. "He is not my prisoner," he yelled. "I will let him go."

"Let him go! You're crazy."

"I'm alive. He saved my life."

"Bah!" The burgomaster's face contorted in contempt. "Sentimentality! It doesn't become you, Hartog. Besides, you gave your word! You swore an oath. Now you must keep it."

The thiefcatcher stood beside Willems, his jaw clenching and unclenching. No one said a word. A wind whipped up, and Hartog was suddenly aware of his wet clothes and a bone-deep chill. Abruptly he turned, grasped Willems by the arm, and pushed him toward a footbridge in the distance. His words snapped in the cold air. "Here he is. Let's be done with this business." A cheer rose from the other shore.

Weeks passed. The thiefcatcher spent more and more time in the alehouse. "Hartog always gets his man!" he shouted more than once in a drunken stupor. In between he muttered into his mug, "Just doing my job." Finally, poverty sobered him up. On a bright spring morning, after sleeping most of a day and a night, he stalked to the burgomaster's office to claim his money.

Pocketing his money and receipt from the clerk, he turned his head toward the courtroom down the hall. Voices rose and fell and there was a loud undercurrent, a room full of wooden benches creaking as bodies shifted. "What's going on?"

"Eh?" The clerk looked up. "Oh. The sentencing of Dirk Willems."

Hartog's feet propelled him toward the heavy wooden doors. A bailiff took a look at him, then jerked his thumb toward a door further down the hall marked "Spectators." He crept in quietly, trying to hide his bulk as he sat on a bench.

Willems was facing the panel of judges, his back to the spectators. One of the judges was reading aloud:

> Whereas Dirk Willems, born at Asperen, at present a prisoner, has confessed, without torture, that before the age of twenty he was rebaptized in Rotterdam at the house of one Pieter Willems. Further, at his house in Asperen, he has harbored secret meetings for worship and admitted to prohibited doctrines. He has also permitted several persons to be rebaptized at his house, all of which is contrary to our holy Christian faith, and to the decrees of his royal majesty, and ought not to be tolerated, but severely punished as an example to others.

The words slowly penetrated Hartog's consciousness. Rebaptism? Secret meetings? This was the man who was so dangerous? The judge was still reading.

Therefore, we judges, having examined and considered
the evidence with grave deliberation, in behalf of his royal
majesty, do condemn the aforesaid Dirk Willems, who
persists obstinately in his opinion, to be executed with
fire until death ensues. All his property shall be
confiscated for the benefit of his royal majesty. So done
this 16th of May, in presence of the judges, A.D. 1569.

The judge rose. "Execution, noon today, outside city
limits." A gavel cracked. "Court dismissed."

Hartog rose woodenly with the others. Death in the fire?
Why death? Does a man die for baptizing and having
meetings? And this was a good man!

The thiefcatcher was not aware of making a conscious
decision to join the crowd gathered just off the road between
Asperen and Leerdam. A stiff east wind blew at his back. He
shivered in spite of the bright sun and pushed his way through
the crowd. He heard a loud cry, a man in agony: "Oh, my Lord!
My God!" (*That same voice, calm, reassuring: "Don't panic,
man. Grab hold! Grab hold!"*)

As he broke through the crowd, he saw Willems chained to
a stake, a roaring fire at his feet. The wind was blowing the
flames away from his body. Seconds became minutes. The
minutes dragged on, punctuated only by Willems' cries, "My
God, my God!" (*"Good, good," the same voice had said. "Don't
fight. Just hang on."*)

"He suffers too much!" yelled the thiefcatcher.

"Yes, yes!" others in the crowd agreed.

The bailiff, watching astride his horse, wheeled the animal
around, then bent down and said something to the
executioner.

Hartog turned away, tears coursing down his face, and
began pushing his way back through the crowd. The cries
suddenly ceased.

❧   ❧   ❧

Contemporary Peacemaker

While hostilities against Iraq increased during the fall of 1990, Mennonites thought about how to show love to the people their government called enemies, the people of Iraq. Christian Peacemaker Teams planned a trip to Iraq. Soon Mennonites and folks from the Church of the Brethren found themselves on the dangerous mission of visiting Iraq, where United States hostages were being held. Would they also be taken hostage? Gerald Hudson is one who decided that loving meant risking the unknown by traveling to Iraq. Read this interview with Gerald, and/or interview a local peacemaker (see questions on page 22):

While I grew up in Mississippi in the 1960s, we were segregated by law. My heart burned with desire to see reconciliation between the races. I was brought up in a Christian home. I lived with my grandmother, a deaconess in the church and the choir director. All the songs were about God's love and how Jesus loves us all, no matter what color we are. I wondered, If God is such a God of love, why can't blacks and whites get together, especially the Christians?

As a child, I had a close, personal relationship with Jesus. I talked to God every day and treated God's Son as my special friend. That carried me through childhood and teen years, and I know it has made me a better adult. I didn't wait until I was grown to think that I could talk to God or ponder the world's problems. You junior youth should see yourselves like the twelve-year-old Jesus, sitting in the temple, wrestling with doctors of the law, and even teaching them. That same spirit is available to twelve-year-old kids today. You can bring simple wisdom, insight, and innocence to important discussions.

When I was in the sixth and seventh grades, we would have race wars. We were angry and frustrated about racism. One time my older brother and I cornered a white guy walking through our neighborhood. My brother hit him and pushed him. I stopped my brother from beating him up and yelled at the top of my voice, "Why do you have to do that? Why do you have to hit him?" I took the white guy down to the neighborhood store so the white owner could take care of him. That was my first step into peacemaking. At school my black friends would sometimes beat up white guys just to show that blacks weren't inferior. I often found myself in the middle of that, trying to stop that, and was called a honky lover, the opposite of a nigger lover. I made those decisions by instinct, just responding out of my own heart.

I had a passion for peace, but also for justice. I was suspended or expelled from school every year, seventh grade through twelfth. I was always fighting against injustice, racism, the power structure. One example: Some kids today wear their hair in braids. We used to do that in the sixties, but when schools were integrated, teachers wouldn't let us wear braids any more. I would say, "This is our culture. This is part of who we are. Our hair is different from yours, and we should be allowed to treat it differently." I would lead protests and would find myself getting suspended.

My trip to Iraq was very interesting. I had always wanted to go to the Middle East, to walk where Jesus walked and get holy goose bumps. But instead, I was on the other side, not in the Promised Land. I went to the Iraqi people to make peace, to be a reconciler. When I got there, I found not only what I expected, Moslems and Shiites, whom God had created. I also

found Christian sisters and brothers of the same faith background that I was. The large Christian community made my trip more meaningful. Here were Christians against whom my country was going into battle. It was important for me to say, "We can settle our differences through nonviolent ways." Somehow, we must more and more keep promoting nonviolent methods of solving our conflicts.

We didn't stop the war, but we weren't a failure. Jesus died on the cross, and what seemed like a failure was probably the greatest triumph in history. Jesus could have called ten thousand angels, he could have overthrown the Roman government, he could have set up his kingdom. Those would have been definitions of success by our standards. Instead, God sent his Son to be faithful, to be willing to die for others. That was why I went to Iraq—not to kill for what I believe, but to be willing to die for what I believed. God calls us to be faithful. If we are faithful, then I think the world will be converted. That's the way God wants to convert the world, not by beating it into submission. So the idea is not to beat Saddam Hussein into submission but to change hearts and make peace.

I enjoy talking with youth, and I give workshops on conflict and racism. Contact me at Eastern Mennonite College, 1200 Park Road, Harrisonburg, VA 22801-2462; phone 703 432-4450.

 Violence ends where love begins.[6]

'If your enemies are hungry,
feed them; if they are thirsty,
give them something to drink;
for by doing this you will heap
burning coals on their heads.'
Do not be overcome by evil,
but overcome evil with good.

Romans 12:20-21

Session 3

We Trust God Alone

Summary: We don't go to war because we do not rely on governments and their armed forces to save us from enemies. We place our trust in God alone.

Memory Verse: *We must obey God rather than any human authority* (Acts 5:29b).

Bible Texts Behind Session 3

Psalm 20:6-8

Matthew 10:18

Matthew 19:19

Acts 5:29

Acts 16–17

Romans 12:1-2, 17-21

Romans 13:1-3, 8-10

2 Corinthians 1:21-22

Revelation 17:14

PART A

Story: We present our bodies as living sacrifices to God.

Faith Focus: We worship only God, who is love. We do not worship the government, who tells us to kill enemies.

Notes to Parents

1. Have you been thinking about your own heroes of love and telling their stories to your youths? Collections of peace stories listed in appendix 3 will provide you with many inspiring models.

2. What does *worship* mean to you? What does it mean to give all of yourself to God? What does it mean for your youths? In children's eyes, how is worship connected to trust?

Youth-Adult Conversation

Adult: When we last met, we discussed how difficult it is to love our enemies. What do you especially remember? Do you have some questions you'd like to discuss before we go on?

Youth: *(May respond.)*

Adult: We also talked about heroes of love. *(Give the name of one of your heroes and tell a bit about that person.)* Who is one of your heroes of love?

Youth: *(May respond.)*

Adult: Do you remember what we said earlier about worshiping God? What did the angels say when they greeted the shepherds?

Youth: "Glory to God in the highest heaven."

Adult: We said that meant God alone is worthy to be worshiped.

Youth: But that's not a problem for me. I don't believe in any of those old-fashioned Roman and Greek gods.

Adult: Neither do I. But we also talked about how the Roman emperors of that time demanded to be worshiped.

Youth: How do you worship a living person?

Adult: Some of these emperors wanted to be called "lord" and "savior," names Christians used only for Jesus. These rulers also wanted citizens to offer sacrifices to them.

Youth: And what happened to those who refused?

Adult: Domitian, who ruled late in the first century, persecuted Christians who refused to call him god. Some
were thrown to the lions, and for fun, some people
watched them being mauled.[1] Many Christians were
thrown in jail.

Youth: But I still don't understand where you're leading. Our
president doesn't ask us to worship *him*.

Adult: No, he has never asked us to offer a sacrifice or bow
before him. But let's think about what *worship* means.
What do you think worship is?

Youth: *(May respond.)*

Adult: *(May respond.)* Let's see how Paul explains worship in Romans.

Youth: "I appeal to you therefore, brothers and sisters, by the mercies of God,

Adult: "to present your bodies as a living sacrifice, holy and acceptable to God, which is your spiritual worship.

Youth: "Do not be conformed to this world, but be transformed by the renewing of your minds, so that you may discern what is the will of God—what is good and acceptable and perfect" (Romans 12:1-2).

Adult: So what is "spiritual worship"? What are we to present?

Youth: *(May respond.)*

Adult: And when we present our bodies, what are we offering?

Youth: *(May respond.)*

Adult: When we present our bodies, we are offering every part of our lives. When we worship God, we offer all that our bodies are and everything we do.[2]

Youth: Then maybe the Sunday morning service helps to remind us of that.

Adult: Good point.

Youth: And how does all this relate to worshiping the president of the United States?

Adult: Worship also has to do with whom we trust. How do you explain trust?

Youth: *(May respond.)*

Adult: *(May respond.)* In some ways, we worship what we trust. Here is the question: To save us from enemies, do we first of all trust God or our president and our country?

Youth: Hmmm. Last time we talked about God wanting us to love our enemies. But our government uses war to kill enemies.

Adult: These are worship choices. Do we choose to worship God and love our enemies, or to follow the government and go to war against our enemies?

Youth: If I worship God, then I don't want the government to protect me with weapons and soldiers and war. But it's scary to be without weapons! Another country might invade and hurt me!

Adult: Yes, it is scary. But let's remember who is in charge here. God will be the winner! Look at Psalm 20.

Youth: "Now I know that the Lord will help his anointed;
he will answer him from his holy heaven
with mighty victories by his right hand.

Adult: "Some take pride in chariots, and some in horses,
but our pride is in the name of the Lord our God.

Youth: "They will collapse and fall,
but we shall rise and stand upright" (Psalm 20:6-8).

Adult: Notice what is said here. Whom will the Lord help?

Youth: His anointed, the king. Can't that mean King Jesus, and all his followers, including me?

Adult: Yes. If you choose to worship God, you are among God's anointed (2 Corinthians 1:21-22).

Youth: And "we shall rise and stand upright" —

Adult: That means us! God will be victorious! And *we* stand with God! What were horses and chariots used for?

Youth: Waging war?

Adult: Right! And what will happen to those who rely on them?

Youth: "They will collapse and fall." Doesn't sound like they will win!

Adult: We rely on God for salvation, and not on our government, which wages war. In times of trouble, we don't call out the marines. Instead, we submit ourselves to God.

Youth: How soon will God's victory come?

Adult: That's a hard question to answer. Revelation talks more about the victory.[3]

Youth: "They will make war on the Lamb, and the Lamb will conquer them, for he is Lord of lords and King of kings, and those with him are called and chosen and faithful" (Revelation 17:14).

Adult: Jesus, the martyred lamb, conquers through "The Word of God," which is like a "sharp, two-edged sword" (Revelation 1:16; 19:11-16). We just don't know when the victory will come. In a sense, when Jesus was raised from the dead, the victory began. Death and destruction had no power over Jesus.

Youth: But if another country invades us. . . .

Adult: This gets quite difficult. Let's think about the worst thing an enemy country could do to us.

Youth: There's nothing worse than being killed, is there?

Adult: I think so. The worst thing is to be separated from the love of God. Forever.

Youth: If I do what God doesn't want me to, if I hate and kill my enemies when the government calls me to do so, that would separate me from God.

Adult: Yes. When you hate and kill, you aren't giving God's love a chance to win. You aren't allowing God to do miracles of love.

Youth: So to follow Jesus, to worship God, I do what God asks, instead of what the government asks. I love my enemies.

Adult: That's what the memory verse says.

All: **"We must obey God rather than any human authority"** (Acts 5:29b).

Adult: This has been lots of heavy talk. Let's review. What is the difference between obeying and trusting God, or obeying and trusting the government telling us to go to war?

Youth: *(May respond.)*

Adult: Before we stop, let's remember that, even if you decide to hate and kill and separate yourself from God, you

can always choose to return to God's way of love. God
will always be glad to have you back.

Youth: I guess learning God's way is a lifelong journey.

Adult: It's a path we *decide* to take, step after step after step.
And the first thing we do when we're starting on a
journey is to prepare ourselves.[4] One of the best ways
for us to do that is talk to God. Let's pray together.

All: **God, we confess that it is hard to worship you alone.
Sometimes we trust other things more than we trust
you. Help us to remember that you will be the winner
in the end and that you are worthy of our highest
trust and worship. Guide our feet on the path to
peace. Amen.**

Notes to Parents

1. How did this section go? The concept of something being worse than death is extremely difficult for children and
youths to grasp. Studies have shown that, during the Cold
War, children feared separation from parents or from someone
who would care for them. That was much more stressful for
children than the fear of death, which they couldn't quite understand. As you continue to process these ideas, emphasize
that God can and will always care for your children and
youths—something the government surely cannot promise!

2. What does it mean to give God's love a chance to win?
What kind of sacrifice might that demand? How do you explain
to youths the willingness to suffer rather than to inflict harm
on another? Have you alerted them about the need to ask for
help from trustworthy adults if they are abused or mistreated?

3. Do you truly believe that the worst thing that could
happen to you is to be separated from God's love? Living out
that belief will take a lifetime of thought and action. Where are
you now on that journey? What step will you take next on the
path of peace?

PART B

Story: Paul chose to obey God rather than the men who told him to stop preaching about Jesus.

Faith Focus: While we are commanded to be subject to the government, we are first of all to be obedient to God.

Notes to Parents

1. Can you give an example your youths will understand of a time you learned to put your trust in God alone? It can be a time when you moved forward in trusting God or a time you trusted something else that failed you. Children and youths find it comforting to know that their parents make mistakes, learn from them, and keep going!

2. Early Christians refused to offer a simple sacrifice to Caesar. Many told them the sacrifice was meaningless and harmless. Yet faithful Christians decided they could not offer the sacrifice after making the promise to worship God alone. They were imprisoned and sometimes killed. Where do you draw the line in obeying the state?

3. *Before* continuing, together read the biblical drama "Peter Disobeys" (see Contents for "Biblical Dramas").

Word List

conscientious objectors   Those who refuse to go to war because their conscience tells them it is wrong

Youth/Adult Conversation

Adult: Last time we discussed difficult ideas. One was the difference between placing our trust in God or in our country. What does it mean to you to trust God?

Youth: *(May respond.)*

Adult: I often have to remind myself what it means to place my trust only in God. *(Give an example of a time when that was difficult.)* Now I have to figure out how to keep growing to trust God more.

Youth: I'm starting to see that for protection, I need to trust God instead of my country's armed forces.

Adult: Last time we also talked about choosing to love our enemies rather than to fight them.

Youth: The government accepts that choice to love enemies. Draft laws say we can be conscientious objectors to war.

Adult: Do you understand what a conscientious objector is, a C.O.? How do you explain it?

Youth: *(May respond.)*

Adult: *(Be sure your youths understand the term.)* Conscientious objectors are those whose conscience won't let them fight. We Christians say our conscience comes from how God guides us.

Youth: Our conscience tells us right from wrong. I learn what is right and wrong from the Bible.

Adult: As you said, the draft laws provide for a person to be a C.O. But they didn't always say that. During World War I there was no legal way to refuse to fight and instead be a C.O.

Youth: What happened to those who didn't want to fight?

Adult: Those who would not fight or wear the army uniform were treated horribly. Some were put in damp cells with only skimpy underwear, no bed to sleep on, and little to eat or drink.

Youth: That happened in the United States?

Adult: Yes. By refusing to "serve their country" and saying they instead chose to follow God's ways, they were accused of not being loyal to their country.

Youth: Are you saying that there are times when we have to choose between worshiping God and obeying our country?

Adult: Yes. *(Explain a difficult choice you've made.)*

Youth: But doesn't the Bible tell us to *obey* the government?

Adult: It tells us to *be subject* to the government. There is a difference. Let's look at Romans.

Youth: "Let every person be subject to the governing authorities; for there is no authority except from God, and those authorities that exist have been instituted by God. Therefore whoever resists authority resists what God has appointed, and those who resist will incur judgment" (Romans 13:1-2).

Adult: Many people claim this text as a basis for how they relate to the government. It tells us to be subject to the government. But being subject is sometimes different from being obedient.

Youth: Uh, where's a dictionary?

Adult: *Obedience* is what we owe God. We are to obey the Ten Commandments, Jesus' teachings, and the leading of the Holy Spirit in our own day. And, whenever our faith allows it, we are to obey the laws of our government.

Youth: Most of the laws I have no trouble obeying and they make good sense, like driving on the right side of the road rather than just anywhere, and building homes safely.

Adult: But might there be laws you'd have trouble obeying?

Youth: I suppose if the government told me I had to kill or hurt someone, I'd have trouble obeying. You didn't explain yet what it means to *be subject.*

Adult: Right. Being subject means to agree that the government has authority over you. Governments keep order, and we are subject to that.

Youth: So being subject means that we don't stop the government from keeping order. Can you explain more?

Adult: If we don't agree with something our government tells us, it is not our task to overthrow the government. It is not even our place to refuse to take our punishment for disagreeing.

Youth: I think I need an example.

Adult: During World War I, those men reported to military camp as ordered, but refused to put on military uniforms or perform military tasks. But they submitted to the punishment the government decided they deserved. They didn't fight back or behave in unloving ways to those who were so unkind.

Youth: So they refused to obey the order to be part of the military, but were subject to the government who then punished them.

Adult: And they tried to show love to those who were being so mean.

Youth: If I continue reading in Romans, that love is emphasized:

"Owe no one anything, except to love one another; for the one who loves another has fulfilled the law.

Adult: "The commandments, 'You shall not commit adultery; You shall not murder; You shall not steal; You shall not covet'; and any other commandment, are summed up in this word, 'Love your neighbor as yourself.'

Youth: "Love does no wrong to a neighbor; therefore, love is the fulfilling of the law" (Romans 13:8-10).

Adult: Paul is quoting Jesus who said, "Love your neighbor as yourself" (Matthew 19:19). If we back up to Romans 12, we find core verses for Christian nonresistance. Remember what nonresistance is?

Youth: *(May respond.)*

Adult: Nonresistance is refusing to be mean back to someone who is mean to you.

Youth: "Do not repay anyone evil for evil, but take thought for what is noble in the sight of all. If it is possible, so far as it depends on you, live peaceably with all.

Adult: "Beloved, never avenge yourselves, but leave room for the wrath of God; for it is written, 'Vengeance is mine, I will repay, says the Lord.'

Youth: "No, 'if your enemies are hungry, feed them; if they are thirsty, give them something to drink; for by doing this you will heap burning coals on their heads.' Do not be overcome by evil, but overcome evil with good" (Romans 12:17-21).

Adult: We use these verses most often to explain why we try to love our enemies.

Youth: Why are those verses about the government sandwiched between such important verses about love?

Adult: Good question! When studying the Bible, it is important to look at the verses before and after a section to get a flow for the author's ideas.

Youth: You mean I shouldn't just pick a verse out of the middle without understanding what else is close by?

Adult: Right. What might Paul, the author of Romans, have had in mind by sticking this section about government between these about love?

Youth: Didn't you say that, about this time, there were some Jews trying to overthrow the government? That wasn't very loving!

Adult: Right! Zealots were arming themselves against the Romans. When Paul wrote this passage, he was afraid that Roman Christians might also be considering rebellion.

Youth: So Paul didn't want the Christians to think they could become Zealots.

Adult: He wanted to remind them that was not God's way and that government does have a function. But he didn't say government has ultimate claim for our obedience, or to obey the government when it makes ungodly demands.

Youth: Didn't Paul spend time in jail for not obeying the government?

Adult: Yes, he did (Acts 16–17), and so did other apostles, including Peter. Our memory verse is taken from a time

We should never forget that everything Adolf Hitler did in Germany was 'legal.'

—*Martin Luther King*[5]

Peter and others had been in jail for preaching about Jesus.

Youth: I remember! An angel came and released them, and they returned to the temple to teach. The high priest again had them arrested and asked why they had disobeyed.

Adult: Let's repeat the verse together which was their answer.

All: **"We must obey God rather than any human authority"** (Acts 5:29b).

Adult: Jesus even warned his disciples that they would have trouble with the government. Read Matthew 10:18.

Youth: "You will be dragged before governors and kings because of me, as a testimony to them and the Gentiles" (Matthew 10:18). Now that I think about it, Jesus had lots of trouble with the government, too. The rulers crucified him!

Adult: So the important thing is to balance the Romans 13 passage with the way Jesus, Paul, and the other early apostles lived. Above all, we want to love, as Christ's followers are called to do.

Youth: But how do I decide when to obey the government and when not?

Adult: Perhaps we need to turn that around. First, we worship God. We make our decisions based on our obedience to Jesus. As we seek to follow the leading of the Holy Spirit, we might find that we can't obey a law. But we are not reacting against the government; we are taking a stand for Jesus.

Youth: As I learn more about following Jesus, my mind will become more clear about the one I worship and trust.
Adult: I think so, too. What's the third reason we don't go to war?
Youth: *(May respond.)*
Adult: Let's pray together.
All: **Lord God, we used the good minds you gave us when we decided to follow you and your way of love. Give us your good judgment as we make daily decisions about what that means. Guide us in the path to peace. Amen.**

Notes to Parents

1. There are other stories in the Bible about those who suffered in jail (or a lion's den) rather than obeying an evil law of the government. As you review this session, see how many of these stories you and your youths can remember.

2. When my children were quite young, I found them playing "jail" with the kitchen cupboard doors. I was aghast until I realized that they knew about jail only through the stories of Joseph and the apostles. Many people in jail today are there for doing wrong. Yet some continue to be there for conscience' sake. How do you feel about people going to prison because they have made a choice to follow God rather than the rules of the government?

3. Can you think of laws you are uncomfortable obeying? There hasn't been a draft since the Vietnam War, and the entire Persian Gulf War was fought without one. However, our money *is* continually being "drafted" to arm our country and prepare for battle. Our money was used to fight the Gulf War. On average, Mennonites pay $9 in war taxes for every $5 they give to the church.[6] How do you feel about that?

> **If a thousand men were not to pay
> their tax bill this year, that would not
> be as violent and bloody a measure as
> it would be to pay them and enable the
> State to commit violence and shed
> innocent blood.**
>
> —*Henry David Thoreau*[7]

4. Many schools believe kindergartners are ready to learn about allegiance to their country, so they teach the pledge to the flag. Perhaps you've heard of young children who end the pledge of allegiance with "Amen." Why might they confuse it with a prayer? What does this say about their understanding of worship?

5. Here is how Susan Clemmer Steiner rewrote the pledge of allegiance:

> **I pledge allegiance
>   to the cross
>   of Jesus Christ,
> And to the forgiveness
>   for which it stands,
> One church under God,
>   indivisible,
> With liberty and
>   justice for all.**[8]

How is this the same as the pledge to the flag or different from it? What does it mean to pledge allegiance to a flag? Many Mennonites, especially in the past, did not say the pledge.

> **War doesn't decide who's right—only
> who's left.**[9]

Historic Peacemaker

World War I was a popular war, and many Christians were sure Jesus wanted them to fight and win it. Problem was, these Christians were on both sides of the war. A favorite German slogan was, *Gott mit uns* (God with us).

In the United States, preachers gave eloquent sermons about how Jesus would be willing to kill the Germans and that American young men should be pleased to do the same.[10] Those who decided not to obey the government's commands were treated with disgust. Four Hutterites reported to military camps as commanded, but they refused to take part when they arrived.

❧ ❧ ❧

Christ or Country?

Titus Peachey and Linda Gehman Peachey[11]

During World War I, conscientious objection to military service was not tolerated in the United States. Conscientious objectors (COs) often obeyed their draft orders and went to military training camps, where their convictions against military involvement obliged them to refuse all military duty. They were frequently mistreated in response. David, Michael, and Joseph Hofer and Jacob Wipf were four young men who chose to risk severe treatment rather than compromise their belief in Christ's way of peace.

All four of these men were Hutterites, members of a communal tradition that grew out of the Anabaptist movement

*in Reformation Europe. During the intense persecution of the
times, that occurred in the early years of the movement, the
Hutterites (named for their founder Jakob Hutter) pooled their
resources so that none would go hungry. They continue to live
communally today.*

As the four Hutterites traveled from their home in South
Dakota to the military camp in Lewis, Washington, their
troubles began right away. The other young men on the train
tried to cut the Hutterites' hair and beards, treating them
roughly and with contempt.

When they arrived at camp, they were asked to sign a card
promising obedience to all military commands. As absolute
objectors to all military service on the basis of their religious
convictions, they refused any service within the military. They
were commanded to line up with the others and march to the
exercise grounds. They refused, and would not accept the
uniform either. They were immediately put in the guardhouse.

After two months in the guardhouse they were court-
martialed and sentenced to thirty-seven years, with a reduced
sentence of twenty years, in the military prison on the island of
Alcatraz.

Chained together two by two, hands and feet, they
traveled under armed guard. By day the fetters on their ankles
were unlocked, but never the handcuffs. At night they had to
lie two by two, flat on their backs, doubly chained together.
They slept little during the two nights of the journey.

When they arrived at Alcatraz, their clothes were taken
from them and they were ordered to put on the military
uniform, which they again refused to do. They were then put
into solitary confinement in dark, dirty, stinking cells. The
uniforms were thrown down next to them with the warning, "If
you don't give in, you'll stay here till you die, like the four we
dragged out of here yesterday." So they were locked up
wearing nothing but their light underwear.

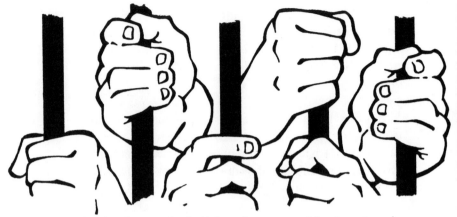

The first four-and-a-half days they got nothing to eat, and only half a glass of water each day. At night they slept on the wet and cold concrete floor without blankets. Their cell was below sea level, and water oozed through the walls.

For the last day-and-a-half they stood with their hands tied together crosswise above their heads and fastened to iron rods so high they could barely touch the floor with their feet. This strained their tendons in their arms so badly that David Hofer said after his release that he could still feel the effects on his sides. He tried to ease the terrible pain by pushing the toilet bucket toward himself with one foot and then standing on it. The four could not speak to each other because they were too far apart, but once David heard Jacob Wipf cry out: "O Almighty God!"

At the end of five days they were brought out of the dungeon into the yard, where a group of other prisoners stood. One of the other prisoners said with tears in his eyes: "Isn't it a shame to treat people like that?" The men were covered with a rash, badly bitten by insects, and their arms so swollen that they could not get their jackets on. They had been beaten with clubs. Michael Hofer was once beaten so severely that he passed out.

They continued to go without food for the fifth day until

supper. After that they were locked up again in their cells day and night. On Sundays they were allowed to walk for an hour in the fenced-in courtyard, but under heavy guard. They spent four months in the prison of Alcatraz this way.

In late November, guarded by six armed sergeants and chained together two by two, they were transferred from Alcatraz to Fort Leavenworth in Kansas. After four days and five nights of travel, they arrived at eleven o'clock one night in Leavenworth, and were loudly driven up the street to the military prison with bayonets, like pigs. Chained together at the wrists, they carried their bags in their free hand and their Bibles and an extra pair of shoes under their arms. By the time they reached the prison gate they were sweating so much that their hair was wet. In this condition, in the raw winter air, they had to take off their clothes in order to put on the prison garb that was to be brought to them. When the clothes finally came two hours later, they were chilled to the bone. Early in the morning, at five o'clock, they again had to stand outside a door in the cold wind and wait. Joseph and Michael Hofer could bear it no longer—they had to be taken to the hospital.

Jacob Wipf and David Hofer were put in solitary confinement because they again refused to take up prison work under military control. Their hands were stretched out through the iron bars and chained together. They stood that way for nine hours a day, getting only bread and water. This lasted two weeks; then they received regular meals for two weeks, and so on alternately.

When the two Hofer brothers became critically ill, Jacob Wipf sent a telegram home to their wives, who left their children and traveled to Kansas the same night, accompanied by a relative. Confusion at the railroad station caused a day's delay, and when they finally reached Fort Leavenworth at eleven o'clock at night, they found their husbands close to death and hardly able to speak.

The next morning, when they were allowed to come in

again, Joseph Hofer was already dead and his body in a coffin. They were told he could not be seen anymore. But his wife, Maria, made her way to the commanding officer in spite of guards and doors and pleaded to see her husband once more. They showed her where the body was. She went and looked through tears into the coffin, but to her horror she saw that her beloved husband had been put into the military uniform he had so valiantly refused to wear while living.

His brother Michael, who died a few days later, was dressed in his own clothes, according to the strongly expressed wish of his father, who had arrived in the meantime. When Michael died, his father, his wife and his brother David were present.

After the relatives had left with the body, David Hofer was returned to his cell and chained. Later he reported, "The whole next day I stood there and wept. I could not even wipe away my tears because my hands were chained to the prison bars." The next morning one of the guards took a message from David to the commanding officer. He asked to have a cell closer to Jacob Wipf, so that they could at least see each other, even if they would not be allowed to speak together. An hour later the guard returned and told David to pack up his things—he had been released!

On December 6, 1918, the Secretary of War issued an order prohibiting the punishment of military prisoners by handcuffing and chaining. But five days later, when two Hutterite brothers visited Jacob Wipf in Fort Leavenworth, they found him still in solitary confinement, his hands chained to the iron bars for nine hours a day, with short breaks for meals. At six each afternoon his chains were taken off. He was given four blankets for the night but had to sleep on the concrete floor.

Jacob Wipf sent the following message home with the visitors: "Sometimes I envy the three who have already been released from this torment. Then I think, why is the hand of the

Lord so heavy upon me? I have always tried to be faithful and hardworking and have hardly ever made any trouble for the brotherhood. Why must I go on suffering all alone? But then there is joy too, when I think that the Lord considers me worthy to suffer for his sake. And I must confess that my life here, compared with our previous experiences at Alcatraz, is like living in a palace."

On December 12, 1918, the chaining of military prisoners was finally discontinued in accordance with the order of the Secretary of War. The solitary prisoners received planks on the floor to sleep on, making it considerably warmer than the bare concrete floor. There were more improvements after Christmas, when the War Department received many petitions on behalf of the prisoners.

Jacob Wipf was finally released on April 13, 1919.

Contemporary Peacemakers

In the spring of 1991, a new junior high was dedicated in Goshen, Indiana. Kelly Short was invited to lead the Pledge of Allegiance at the service. Read this interview with Kelly, and/or interview a local peacemaker (see questions on page 22):

Sadako and the Thousand Paper Cranes is a book that influenced my

peace stance. It personalized war for me. Sadako was a young person directly affected by the dropping of the atom bomb on Japan.

When I decided not to lead the pledge at the dedication of my junior high building, I was a strong Christian and supported by my church community, pastors, and youth group.

I told my principal that my allegiance was to God, not to the flag and not to the United States. He understood and respected the decision.

If I had said the pledge, it would have shown that nationalism or patriotism were important to me. Instead, I believed in God and was a pacifist. Showing allegiance to a nation at war would be indirectly supporting the war, and I wouldn't want to be seen doing that. It wasn't a hard decision.

Now I also see the practical side of peace. We can't go on with wars if we are going to survive. I try to live a peaceful and peacemaking life as much as possible.

I'd be glad to talk to you and your Sunday school class about making peace. Contact me at 2612 Martin Manor Drive, Goshen, IN 46526; phone 219 533-4598.

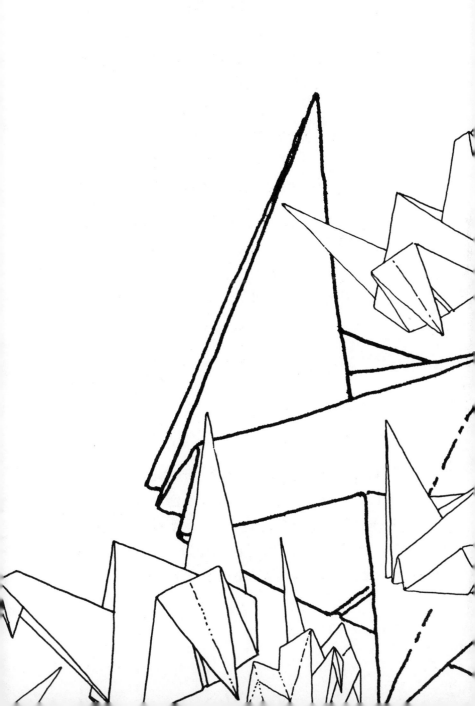

The wolf shall live with the lamb,
the leopard shall lie down
with the kid,
the calf and the lion and the
fatling together,
and a little child shall lead them.

The cow and the bear shall graze,
their young shall lie down
together;
and the lion shall eat straw
like the ox.

The nursing child shall play
over the hole of the asp,
and the weaned child shall put
its hand on the adder's den.

They will not hurt or destroy
on all my holy mountain;
For the earth will be full of the
knowledge of the Lord
as the waters cover the sea.

Isaiah 11:6-9

Session 4

Peace Is
God's Vision

Summary: We don't go to war because God's ideal, already in the Old Testament, is a peaceable kingdom.

Memory Verse: *They shall beat their swords into plowshares, and their spears into pruning hooks; nation shall not lift up sword against nation, neither shall they learn war any more* (Isaiah 2:4b).

Bible Texts Behind Session 4

1 Chronicles 28:2-3, 6	Isaiah 53:3a
Ezra 8:21-23	Isaiah 58:6-7
Micah 4:1-5	Matthew 11:27
Isaiah 2:4b	Luke 4:21b
Isaiah 9:6-7	Luke 13:18-19
Isaiah 11:6-9	John 1:18

PART A

Story: God's original plan did not include a king for the

Israelites. Under kings, the prophets continued to
explain God's way of peace.

Faith Focus: God was, is, and always will be the same. Jesus,
who lived as a peacemaker, is the fullest revelation of
God.

Notes to Parents

1. Christians don't agree about why God's people sometimes used war in the Old Testament and why Jesus told us to
love our enemies in the New (Matthew 5:43-48). Here is a sim-
plification of four understandings:[1]

a. *Two dispensations:* Jesus brought a new way. God has
led us from primitive "eye for an eye" vengeance to a new
way of love (Exodus 21:23-24; Matthew 5:38-42).

b. *Permissive will:* Guy F. Hershberger in *War, Peace,
and Nonresistance* says that God didn't want to use war to
conquer the Promised Land (Exodus 23:28; Joshua 24:12).
But "as a concession to 'the hardness of your hearts,' "
God allowed killing (see Matthew 19:8 for the principle).

c. *Holy war:* In *Yahweh Is a Warrior,* Millard Lind explains that God fought through miracles (as in Exodus 14-
15). God wanted to be the warrior-king of Israel, but the
people begged for a human king. Kings did not depend on
God to fight. God then used the prophets to explain the
way of peace and point the way to the Messiah.

d. *Two voices:* Ray Gingerich says that "the Old Testament does not speak with a single voice. We, like Jesus,
must decide whether we will read the Old Testament
through the eyes of the prophets or the eyes of the kings.
Jesus read the Scriptures through the eyes of the prophets."

2. *Before* this session, read "Israel Begs for a King" (see
Contents under "Biblical Dramas").

Youth-Adult Conversation

Adult: Last time we talked about worshiping and trusting only God. Do you remember the Bible verse we learned? Let's say it together.

All: *(May respond.)*

Adult: What do you remember learning from the story of Peter in jail?

Youth: *(May respond.)*

Adult: Do you have any other questions?

Youth: *(May respond.)* This time I want to start with some questions!

Adult: Good idea! What do you wonder?

Youth: Why was it okay for David to kill Goliath, but not for us to kill today? That young man of God standing against a giant bully has always excited me.

Adult: What especially attracts you?

Youth: I wonder whether I would have the same courage to face a giant with just a few stones and a slingshot.

Adult: David considered himself a man of war as well as a man of God. As king he led Israel into battle after battle.

Youth: Does that mean that it was okay to make war in the Old Testament?

Adult: Let's talk about that. War in the Old Testament has

long troubled those who believe Jesus is the Prince of Peace. It's been a puzzle.

Youth: Earlier we decided Jesus came to bring peace. I know Jesus came from God. How could God make war in the Old Testament and then send Jesus to make peace? That doesn't make sense!

Adult: It most certainly does not. God is always the same, and Jesus came to show us more about God. We call Jesus the "fullest revelation of God" (see John 1:18).

Youth: Which means?

Adult: What do you think?

Youth: *(May respond.)*

Adult: Jesus said, "No one knows the Father except the son" (Matthew 11:27). Jesus knows more about God than anyone else. One of the reasons Jesus came was to teach us, through the model of his own life, how to live as God wants us to.

Youth: And Jesus lived as a peacemaker, letting others hurt him rather than getting even. But that doesn't explain war in the Old Testament!

Adult: Let's keep putting pieces in the puzzle. At the beginning of our study, we realized that people have different ideas about war today.

Youth: Maybe people in the Old Testament also couldn't agree!

Adult: Good point. The Old Testament has two views of history. Let's back up in Israel's history to the first time the Israelites asked for a king.

Youth: We read about Samuel. God was their king. It certainly wasn't God's idea for the Israelites to have a human king!

Adult: No. God wanted the people to rely on God alone.

Youth: But the people preferred a human king to lead them into battle.

Adult: So, if having a king was not God's original will for them,

Youth: Then perhaps the battles were also not God's favorite idea? We read about that last time in Psalm 20. God's people should rely on God rather than on horses and chariots.

Adult: Let's also read about Ezra. He lead Jews back to Jerusalem after the temple had been rebuilt. This passage is at the beginning of the trip back.

Youth: "Then I proclaimed a fast there, at the river Ahava, that we might deny ourselves before our God, to seek from him a safe journey for ourselves, our children, and all our possessions.

Adult: "For I was ashamed to ask the king for a band of soldiers and cavalry to protect us against the enemy on our way, since we had told the king that the hand of our God is gracious to all who seek him, but his power and wrath are against all who forsake him.

Youth: So we fasted and petitioned our God for this, and he listened to our entreaty" (Ezra 8:21-23).

Adult: Ezra was a scribe of the law and well known, even by the pagan king, for following God's laws.

Youth: And Ezra decided not to use soldiers to protect him.

Adult: I said there are perhaps two views of history in the Old Testament. One is the kings' view about glorious battles. The other is the prophets' view.

Youth: What vision of history did the prophets have?

Adult: Let's look at Isaiah's writings. The New Testament often quotes Isaiah rather than Kings. This familiar passage prophesied Jesus.

Youth: "For a child has been born for us, a son given to us;

Youth: "Authority rests upon his shoulders; and he is named

Youth: "Wonderful Counselor, Mighty God, Everlasting Father, Prince of Peace.

Adult: "His authority shall grow continually, and there shall be endless peace for the throne of David and his kingdom.

Someday they'll give a war and nobody will come.

—*Carl Sandburg*[2]

Youth: "He will establish and uphold it with justice and with righteousness from this time onward and forevermore. The zeal of the Lord of hosts will do this" (Isaiah 9:6-7).

Adult: What vision do you see from Isaiah here?

Youth: *(May respond.)*

Adult: Let's be sure to notice that Jesus will bring justice as well as peace. We'll speak more about justice next time. For now let's remember that the vision of Jesus' coming includes bringing justice.

Youth: What else does Isaiah have to say?

Adult: Isaiah also has a famous passage you mentioned earlier.

Youth: "He was despised and rejected by others; a man of suffering and acquainted with infirmity" (Isaiah 53:3a). I said that?

Adult: You mentioned that Jesus didn't seek revenge, but allowed others to hurt him. Isaiah called this being a "suffering servant."

Youth: Like the stories we've been reading! Christians are not eager to suffer. But they accept suffering for Christ rather than taking revenge and making others suffer.

Adult: Yes. And yet, children and youths who are mistreated need to ask for help from trustworthy adults. Our Bible memory verse is one last vision of peace from Isaiah. Let's repeat that together.

All: **"They shall beat their swords into plowshares, and their spears into pruning hooks; nation shall not lift up sword against nation,**

neither shall they learn war any more"
(Isaiah 2:4b).

Adult: Let's pray.

All: **"Gracious God,**
Give us a heart for simple things:
Love and laughter, bread and wine, tales and dreams.
Fill our lives with green, growing hope.
Make us a people of justice
   whose song is alleluia,
   whose sign is peace,
   and whose name breathes love. Amen." [3]

Notes to Parents

1. How are these sessions going? Do your youths look forward to these times of searching for God's truth together, or do they dread them? Look at the appendixes for ideas to make this time more profitable. Also, review your "Learning Goals" in the Introduction "For Adults."

2. Continue to draw your youths to faith in God by recounting times when God saved peoples out of situations that seemed impossible. This happened in the Old Testament, the New Testament, and throughout church history. We talked before about how loving enemies is a way to let God's miracles take place. Miracles don't always rescue God's people, however. How do you explain that to your youths? What purposes are served by the deaths of martyrs?

Part B

Story: The Old Testament vision of peace was fulfilled in Jesus.

Faith Focus: Because we know Jesus, we work to bring more peace to the world.

Notes to Parents

1. How do you define the Old Testament vision of peace? What does God's justice mean to you? How is your family working to bring this justice to the world? What else might you involve your youth in doing for justice?

2. *Salaam* is Arabic for peace. A similar term, *shalom,* is the Hebrew word for peace in the Old Testament, and many use that term to mean a peace which includes much more than lack of war. Today Arabs who have suffered much under the state of Israel, object to the term. Suad Wakim Kesler, a Christian from Lebanon who now lives in the United States, explains: "The Israeli invasion of Lebanon was called 'Shalom for Galilee.' Well over 19,000 Lebanese and Palestinians were killed. . . . For me, *shalom* stands for American F-16 and phosphorus bombs dropped by Israeli soldiers on Lebanon. It means a deliberate burning of my parents' home. A total fragmentation of Lebanon."[4] Out of respect for these Arab sisters and brothers, I have chosen to redefine *peace* rather than to use the Hebrew word *shalom.*

3. This part refers to the quotation from Menno Simons in the first session. You may want to reread that before beginning.

Youth-Adult Conversation

Adult: We started session 4 by saying there are different ways to look at war in the Old Testament. One was to look at the wars through the eyes of kings. What did we learn about the kings?

Youth: *(May respond.)*

Adult: *(Add something you learned.)* Another way to work with war in the Old Testament is to look at the many passages dealing with peace.

Youth: We already listed some of the peacemakers in the Old Testament when we talked about loving enemies: Joseph, Abraham, and Isaac.

Adult: Your friend, David, also learned a hard lesson about
God's peace. His dream had been to build a temple for
God. Let's read some of his last words from 1 Chroni-
cles 28.

Youth: "Then King David rose to his feet and said: 'Hear me,
my brothers and my people. I had planned to build a
house of rest for the ark of the covenant of the Lord,
for the footstool of our God; and I made preparations
for building.

Adult: " 'But God said to me, "You shall not build a house for
my name, for you are a warrior and have shed
blood. . . .

Youth: " '[God] said to me, "It is your son Solomon who shall
build my house and my courts, for I have chosen him
to be a son to me, and I will be a father to him" ' "
(1 Chronicles 28:2-3, 6).

Adult: David was one of God's beloved. But he had killed
many people, so God didn't let him build the temple.

Youth: That must have been hard for David to understand.

Adult: It is still hard for us to understand. Many think God's
original plan was for peace, but that the people of God
just didn't hear that message well until after Jesus explained it to them again.

Youth: And many still don't hear that message!

Adult: Yes. Let's look at some of those Old Testament passages in which God proclaims that peace is God's way.
Let's concentrate on the prophets' vision of peace.

Youth: I know a vision of peace in the Old Testament! Where
is the passage about the lion and lamb lying down together?

Adult: I think if the Bible had been written in English, we
might be able to find a passage like that.

Youth: You mean it's not in the Bible?

Adult: No. The Old Testament was first written in Hebrew.
Isaiah, who wrote that passage, didn't know that *lion*

and *lamb* would sound so wonderful together in English. He chose to place a wolf and lamb together, and a calf with the lion. Let's read the passage.

Youth: "The wolf shall live with the lamb,
the leopard shall lie down with the kid,
the calf and the lion and the fatling together,
and a little child shall lead them.

Adult: "The cow and the bear shall graze,
their young shall lie down together;
and the lion shall eat straw like the ox.

Youth: "The nursing child shall play over the hole of the asp,
and the weaned child shall put
its hand on the adder's den.

Adult: "They will not hurt or destroy
on all my holy mountain;

Youth: "For the earth will be full of the knowledge of the Lord
as the waters cover the sea" (Isaiah 11:6-9).
It makes me think of Christmas cards!

Adult: That's a wonderful connection! Why do we think of Christmas cards when we hear this passage?

Youth: *(May respond.)*

Adult: *(May add ideas about the little child leading them.)*
One of my favorite visions of God's peace comes from Micah, and part of it is our memory verse.

Youth: But our memory verse is from Isaiah!

Adult: True. It's found twice in the Bible.

Youth: "In days to come
the mountain of the Lord's house
shall be established as the highest of the mountains,
and shall be raised up above the hills.
Peoples shall stream to it,
and many nations shall come and say:

Adult: " 'Come, let us go up to the mountain of the Lord,
to the house of the God of Jacob;

that he may teach us his ways
and that we may walk in his paths.'
For out of Zion shall go forth instruction,
and the word of the Lord from Jerusalem.
He shall judge between many peoples,
and shall arbitrate between strong nations far away;

All: **"They shall beat their swords into plowshares,
and their spears into pruning hooks;
nation shall not lift up sword against nation,
neither shall they learn war any more;**

Youth: "But they shall all sit under their own vines
and under their own fig trees,
and no one shall make them afraid;
for the mouth of the Lord of hosts has spoken.

Adult: "For all the peoples walk,
each in the name of [their] god,

Youth: "But we will walk in the name of the Lord our God
forever and ever" (Micah 4:1-5).
Didn't Menno Simons say something like that in the
first session?

Adult: I guess it was a favorite passage of his also! Which part
did he use?

Youth: *(May respond.)*

Adult: These verses tie the absence of war with having plenty, not being afraid, and walking with God. Where do
you see these ideas linked?

Youth: *(May respond.)* That sounds like more than peace.

Adult: In a way, yes. God's vision of peace in the Old Testament meant much more than no war. It combined
love and justice.

Youth: But what does it mean to combine love and justice?

Adult: The Old Testament vision of peace meant everyone
would have what they needed for a good life. What
might that include?

Youth: *(May respond.)*

Adult: *(Add as suitable.)* When everyone has what they need, there is justice. War often comes from injustice, when some people have more than they need and others have less.

Youth: So in God's perfect vision of peace, there is no war, and people don't want to go to war because they already have enough.

> **God's Shalom, peace, involves inevitably righteousness, justice, wholeness, fullness of life, participation in decision making, laughter, joy, compassion, sharing, and reconciliation.**
> *—Desmond M. Tutu*[5]

Adult: Yes. This idea is important to God. Isaiah explains the worship God prefers as getting rid of what is not justice and making more justice. Let's read from Isaiah. He uses the word "fast" much as today we use the word worship.

Youth: "Is not this the fast I choose:
to loose the bonds of injustice. . . .
Is it not to share your bread with the hungry,
and bring the homeless poor into your house;
when you see the naked, to cover them,
and not to hide yourself from your own kin?"
(Isaiah 58:6-7).

Adult: To bring justice, we have to do more than just feed the hungry. We have to find out why they are hungry and change the root of the problem.

Youth: Is it our job to bring justice?

Adult: God is saying it is the obligation of those who want to

worship God. Can you think of ways our family does
that?

Youth: *(May respond.)*

Adult: Maybe we need to think about where our family sees
injustice and then how we can work to overcome it.
*(Discuss where in the world you see injustice—the
hungry, the homeless on the streets, jobless, etc.)* We'll
talk more about being peacemakers and bringing
more justice in session 6.

Youth: Doesn't this Isaiah text sound a little like Luke 4,
from the first session, where Jesus explained his mission?

Adult: An important connection! What did that passage say?

Youth: *(May respond.)*

Adult: The prophets often spoke about the coming reign of
peace. But this reign did not yet occur in Old Testament days.

Youth: Then along came Jesus, who read a biblical passage
about the reign of peace and said, "Today this scripture has been fulfilled in your hearing" (Luke 4:21b).
Yet there certainly isn't peace around the world today!

Adult: No. In fact, in 1987 there were about 26 wars around
the world. In 1991, at the end of the Cold War between the U.S. and U.S.S.R., there were 14.[6]

Youth: And there are millions of people who are hungry, who
don't have clean drinking water or good medical care.
Why didn't Jesus bring the reign of peace?

Adult: Jesus doesn't force people, just like God didn't force
the people of Israel not to use horses.

Youth: Maybe we can't have a complete reign of peace until
everyone chooses to follow Jesus and make more justice.

Adult: Do you remember the parable of the mustard seed?
(Luke 13:18-19).

Youth: *(May respond.)* We studied that in Bible school one

year, and my teacher showed me a mustard seed. It's
tiny!

Adult: But, as the parable explains, it grows into a tree, and
birds can make nests in the branches. What might
that explain about God's kingdom, the kingdom of
peace?

Youth: *(May respond.)*

Adult: To me it means that even though the kingdom seems
small now, it will someday be mighty.

Youth: Is *mighty* the right word for a kingdom of peace?

Adult: Good point! How do you now answer your question,
"Why was it okay for David to kill Goliath, but not for
us to kill today?"

Youth: *(May respond.)*

Adult: *(May review kingship, suffering, God's vision of peace,
and Jesus' coming to fulfill the reign of peace.)*

Adult: These are difficult ideas.

Youth: I used to think studying the Old Testament was bor-
ing. But lots of fascinating things happened to God's
people! It takes a long time to sort out what God is trying to tell us.

Adult: Maybe that's why Christians disagree about how to
live God's way. Keep reading and studying until you
know for yourself God's vision for peace. Beating
swords into plowshares is a good place to start.

Youth: Except that today we'd have to turn bombs and war-
planes into . . . tractors!

Adult: So what is the fourth reason we don't go to war?

Youth: *(May respond.)*

Adult: Let's pray.

All: **"O Spirit of God, great spirit of peace, pour out upon
your daughters and sons visions and dreams of peace.
Give us hope and confidence, knowing you are our
strength and peace, going before us to show the way.
Amen."**[7]

Notes to Parents

1. Here are other passages where Jesus talks of fulfilling Old Testament prophecy about the reign of peace: Luke 7:22; 11:20; 17:21.

2. As we mentioned in the third session, some feel wars fought today are God's holy wars, and in WW I such claims were made on both sides of the battlefields. Here is a passage written by Albert C. Dieffenbach, editor of *The Christian Register*, during WW I. What are some of your reactions? What do you agree with? disagree with? What makes you uncomfortable? Is this your image of God?

> As Christians, of course, we say Christ approves [of the war]. But would he fight and kill? . . . There is not an opportunity to deal death to the enemy that [Christ] would shirk from or delay in seizing! He would take bayonet and grenade and bomb and rifle and do the work of deadliness against that which is the most deadly enemy of his Father's kingdom in a thousand years. . . . That is the inexorable truth about Jesus Christ and this war; and we rejoice to say it.[8]

3. Guide your family's worship of God to lead the action in bringing justice. Look over the project list for some ideas or glance over session 6.

Historic Peacemaker

The early church, so near in time to Jesus, did not believe Christians should be soldiers. We find no record of Christians in the Roman army until the year 173, when some were part of the "Thundering Legion." There are several possible explanations for Christians choosing not to be soldiers:

1. Soldiers were required to make sacrifices to the emperor, and Christians considered this idolatry.

2. The Roman government often persecuted Christians.

This made Christians unwilling to serve in the army which persecuted their church.

3. The early church thought Jesus would soon return and had no time for being soldiers. They chose instead to spread the good news of Jesus.

4. The army was volunteer. Many new Christians were slaves, freedmen, and women, who were ineligible.

Those who continue to follow Jesus' way of peace think the most important reason early Christians weren't in the army is that Jesus said, "Love your enemies," and lived that way.

Not everyone understood this idea of Christians. In March of the year 295, Fabius Victor decided to celebrate the twenty-first birthday of his cherished son, Maximilianus, with the greatest honor possible—giving his name to the military recruiter. Little did Fabius realize what this would mean.

❧ ❧ ❧

I Cannot Do Evil
Maximilianus

Cornelia Lehn[9]

There was great rejoicing in the house of Fabius Victor. They were celebrating the twenty-first birthday of Maximilianus, Fabius Victor's son. And what a fine young man he was! His father was very proud of him. Maximilianus was not only tall and handsome, he also had a great deal of common sense. Fabius was sure he would make a good soldier and be promoted in no time at all. Fabius had already mentioned his name to Dion, the proconsul of Africa.

At the height of the birthday celebrations, Fabius came out with the main surprise.

"Here, Son," he said, "I have had a special coat made for

you. You will need it when you enlist in the army." Fabius hung the coat around his son's shoulders.

The guests were so busy exclaiming about the handsome coat that they did not notice how quiet Maximilianus had become. Nobody noticed, that is, except his father. Fabius had looked forward to surprising his son with the coat. He thought he would be very excited about it.

"What is the matter, Son?" asked Fabius. "Don't you like the coat?"

"Oh yes, yes, of course," replied Maximilianus, drawing his father aside. "What bothers me is that you assume that I will enlist in the army. As you know, I have become a Christian. My Lord bids me love my enemies. How then can I become a soldier? It is impossible!"

Fabius was shocked. "But, Son, I didn't think that your becoming a Christian would make any difference. I knew you always wanted to become a soldier. As a recruiter for the proconsul's army, I have already given Dion your name. You will need to report to him tomorrow."

"If I must report, I must. But I will not become a soldier," replied Maximilianus with his usual determination.

Fabius sighed. Slowly it dawned on him that this situation could become very dangerous. To be a Christian was extremely unpopular. He knew Maximilianus would, with his usual straightforward truthfulness, admit he was a Christian. What would Dion do? Fabius shuddered, and tried to put the thought out of his mind.

The next morning father and son were on their way to see the proconsul, Dion. There had always been a very good relationship between Fabius and his son. How often they had walked together through fields and woods in happier, carefree days!

"Son," said Fabius brokenly, "I am sorry I mentioned your name as a recruit. I would give anything to undo what I did."

"I know, Father," said Maximilianus. "I do not hold it against you. But you understand, don't you, why I cannot become a soldier?"

"Yes," said Fabius. "I understand that if you take Christ's command to love your enemies seriously, you can't do otherwise."

After a strong handclasp, they continued on their way.

Dion consented to see them immediately. "Welcome, welcome!" he cried jovially. "I must congratulate you, Fabius Victor! You have a fine son."

Then, turning to a table nearby, Dion picked up a soldier's badge. "Maximilianus," he said, "here is your badge. Wear it with honor and courage."

Maximilianus did not step forward to receive the badge from Dion's hand. "I am sorry, Sir," he said, "but I cannot serve as a soldier. I am a Christian and must obey Christ as my sovereign Lord."

The smile faded from Dion's face. "I can't believe my ears," he said. "This is ridiculous. To be a soldier and to serve your country is the most honorable thing you can do. I have heard about these stupid Christians. Surely a fine, intelligent young man like you won't let imaginary religious scruples stand in the way of a brilliant career. Here, take the badge, and I will forget that you are a Christian."

"No," said Maximilianus. "I cannot serve as a soldier. I cannot do evil."

"But I am told there already are Christians in the army and they serve," cried Dion in exasperation.

"They know what is fitting for them," replied Maximilianus, "but I am a Christian and I cannot do evil."

"Evil!" exploded Dion. "Evil! What evil do they do who serve?"

"You know what soldiers do," said Maximilianus, looking straight into Dion's eyes. "They not only kill one man, as a murderer does, but thousands. A crime, multiplied, does not become a virtue."

Dion looked down.

Then he said, "Fabius, you are a recruiter for our army. You know the laws. Persuade your son to change his mind. He must. Otherwise there is only the death penalty."

Fabius became pale. "No," he said. "Even if I could change his mind, I would not. I am proud of my son."

"Then away with you," shouted Dion angrily. At a signal from him, his guards took Maximilianus into custody, and Fabius had to leave the proconsul's chambers.

In agony Fabius walked the streets. "My son, my son," he moaned.

The next morning Maximilianus was executed. On that

day, March 12, 295, he became a martyr for Jesus rather than a soldier in the Roman army.

Soon Fabius discovered how deeply the Christian church in Africa was moved by his son's death. As a special honor, the body was brought to Carthage and buried near the tomb of Cyprianus, a great leader in the church, who had also died as a martyr.

The house of Fabius had become silent. But Fabius rejoiced that his son had remained true. "What a son!" he thought. "What a gift to the Lord!"

❧ ❧ ❧

Contemporary Peacemakers

Cathy and André Gingerich Stoner were Mennonite Central Committee (MCC) workers in Germany during the Persian Gulf War. Their work was on a large U.S. military base, counseling soldiers who decided not to go to war. Read this interview with the

Stoners, and/or interview a local peacemaker (see questions on page 22):

Cathy: When I was in kindergarten, my favorite Sunday school teacher told the story of Zacchaeus the tax collector. At first I just thought about a short, little man in a tree. Later I realized that though everybody in the crowd that day thought Zacchaeus was the bad guy, Jesus went out to eat with him and gave him a chance to change his ways.

André: During grade school I remember watching the news

on TV each night and hearing reports about how many people died in the war in Vietnam that day. My mom and dad watched with me, and we talked about it together. I couldn't imagine Jesus killing anybody. I knew then that war was wrong.

Cathy: Our family had five kids, all close in age, and I was right in the middle. Naturally there were lots of squabbles among us, and I ended up playing the role of peacemaker, trying to make sure people were getting along. I was proud of doing this, but sometimes I felt like I couldn't say what *I* wanted. I also simply avoided conflict when it got too scary. If there was a big fight, I would go somewhere else so I wouldn't get involved.

André: In Germany we met lots of young men and women in the U.S. military, and we learned to see the face above the uniform. While some of these soldiers believed it was their duty to kill the enemy, most were just looking for a job and believed the promises the recruiters made them. I found out that these people liked to sing, play games, and have cookouts just like I do. They love their families and homes like I do. But I also discovered that the military has clever and powerful ways to make them stop treating others like humans. From the first day of basic training, soldiers everywhere are taught one thing—to obey orders, no matter how awful or stupid they might be.

Cathy: Some soldiers we met reminded me of Zacchaeus. When they were ordered to fight in the Persian Gulf War, some of them climbed up over the crowd and looked around. They changed their ways, quit their military jobs, and decided to work for peace. It took guts for them to say no to killing while they were still in the military during a war. They were the real heroes. We were happy to be their friends.

Cathy and André: We would be happy to meet with you to talk about peacemaking and saying no to war. You may contact us through MCC, Box 500, Akron, PA 17501-0500; telephone 717 859-1151.

Lead me from death to life,
from falsehood to truth.
Lead me from despair to hope,
from fear to trust.
Lead me from hate to love,
from war to peace.
Let peace fill our heart,
our world,
our universe.
Amen.

Session 5

God Created All Peoples

Summary: We don't go to war because God created all peoples, and because Jesus lived, died, and was raised to save all peoples and teach them to love each other.

Memory Verse: *You will be my witnesses in Jerusalem, and in all Judea and Samaria, and to the ends of the earth* (Acts 1:8b).

Bible Texts Behind Session 5

Genesis 1:27   Acts 1:8
Matthew 5:23-24   Acts 10
Luke 2:10-11   Ephesians 2:13-18

PART A

Story: God created people with some similar characteristics and some different ones. Jesus came for all peoples.

Faith Focus: We are uneasy around people different from us, but Jesus came to take away that fear and help us to love all kinds of peoples.

Notes to Parents

1. What have you learned to love and appreciate from others you consider different from yourself? How has your family experienced the worldwide family of God? What new experiences do you anticipate?

2. What fears do you have of people you think are different from you? How do you overcome such apprehensions?

3. This session deals with racism. Before beginning, think about your community and the racism evident there. Do minorities have equal opportunities in education, employment, and housing? In the wake of the 1992 Los Angeles riots and a beating death in Detroit, none of us can bury our heads and not face this issue squarely. Be able to discuss with your youths recent events as evidence of racism.

4. This session mentions pizza as a favorite food. If it is enjoyed by your family, you might want to consider serving it this evening.

Youth-Adult Conversation

Adult: We have completed four sessions so far. I can think of at least four reasons we don't go to war. *(Name one.)* Which do you remember?

Youth: *(May respond.)*

Adult: *(Add others.)* Now let's briefly return to what the angel first said to the shepherds. Please read that section from Luke.

Youth: "Do not be afraid; for see—I am bringing you good news of great joy for all the people: to you is born this day in the city of David a Savior, who is the Messiah, the Lord" (Luke 2:10-11).

Adult: Earlier we discussed fears and how Jesus came to take them away. Often we are afraid of people we think are different from us.

Youth: Sometimes I just can't understand why people can't be more the same!

Adult: I remember a line from a song in *My Fair Lady.* "Why can't a woman be more like a man?"

Youth: That's what I mean! Why can't we all be more the same? Why can't pizza be everyone's favorite food? Why can't sweats be the national costume for all countries?

Adult: That's an interesting idea. How would that make things easier for us?

Youth: Maybe we'd understand each other better, and there wouldn't be so many disagreements. That would please God!

Adult: There are some things that are the same about most everyone. Can you think of some?

Youth: Well, I think everyone who has a chance to taste pizza likes it.

Adult: There are a few things the same about everyone besides how they feel about pizza!

Youth: Okay, okay. *(May respond.)*

Adult: *(Add others.)*

Youth: Everyone gets hungry. And cold. And maybe even lonely.

The things that make us alike are stronger than the things that make us different.

—*Jane Addams*[1]

Adult: And when skin of any color gets scratched, blood comes out.

Youth: And the blood is always the same color!

Adult: I think God gave each of us some needs that are the same so that there is always something we can understand about another person. You crave pizza when you are hungry. Other people get hungry also, but what they want to eat may be different.

Youth: I'm still uneasy around people I don't understand.

Adult: What are some things that make you uncomfortable?

Youth: *(May respond.)*

Adult: *(Explain some of your own fears.)* Perhaps that uneasiness is a bit like fear.

Youth: We talked in that first session about Jesus coming to take away fears that lead to war.

Adult: Sometimes when we don't understand people and what they think and do, we find it hard to trust them. When we stop trusting them, it's not long until we get angry enough at them to let them be our enemies. This can lead to racism.

> **Join the Army: travel to exotic, distant lands; meet exciting, unusual people—and kill them.**[2]

Youth: What is racism?

Adult: Discrimination or prejudice based on race.

Youth: Like believing one race is better than another?

Adult: Exactly. Can you think of some forms of racism in our community? *(Give an example.)*

Youth: *(May respond.)*

It is we human beings who have made pigmentation a leprosy in our lives instead of a gift.

—Anonymous[3]

Adult: Racism is a sin, and our job as Christians is to speak out against racism. When I hear or see something racist, especially around you, I will not stay silent.

Youth: I'm glad I'm not racist!

Adult: Perhaps we shouldn't say that so lightly. Most everyone has some prejudice against other peoples. I don't think we should pretend we don't have those feelings at all and keep them bottled up inside.

Youth: Then what should we do?

Adult: We need to examine our own prejudices, think about ways to change those attitudes, and then put ourselves in a situation to make that change.[4]

Youth: That's complicated!

Adult: It certainly is. But allowing racism to continue within ourselves or our neighborhoods is not acceptable for us as Christians.

Youth: So why did God make us all so different?

Adult: Let's look back at Genesis for a clue.

Youth: "So God created humankind in his image, in the image of God he created them; male and female he created them" (Genesis 1:27).

Adult: Since we are created in God's image, I like to think that each unique person reflects the vastness of God's imagination.

Youth: I never thought about God having an imagination.

Adult: Just think what an awesome mind God has to be able to plan how to form so many different noses. Billions and billions of them through the ages!

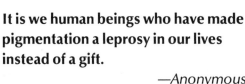

Youth: That's nothing. I wonder how God came up with people who don't like pizza!

Adult: Every time I learn a little more about another culture, I get a glimpse of the magnificence of God's nature and how Jesus and love can reach all peoples.

Youth: Like the angel said, "great joy for all the people."

Adult: And at the end of Jesus' time on earth, he repeated the idea that his coming was for everyone. Let's repeat our memory verse.

All: **"You will be my witnesses in Jerusalem, in all Judea and Samaria, and to the ends of the earth"** (Acts 1:8b).

Youth: I guess if I'm witnessing for Jesus all around the world, I better not kill off the people to whom I'm witnessing. That would defeat the purpose!

Adult: So what are you saying about war?

Youth: Jesus came for all peoples, and my job is to witness to all peoples, even if they are different from me and make me uneasy.

> **The love of one's country is a splendid thing. But why should love stop at the border?**
>
> —*Pablo Casals* [5]

Adult: That's a good place to stop for now. Let's pray.

All: **God, you created a multitude of peoples who understand and worship you in many different ways. Help us to see differences as part of your greatness. Thank you for sending Jesus to help us not be afraid of people who are different from us. Guide us on your path to peace. Amen.**

Notes to Parents

1. In his book *People*, Peter Spier [6] has a picture of a dreary street with all the buildings the same, the cars and buses identical, and everyone looking like an exact replica of everyone else. The next illustration shows the hustle, bustle, and confusion of a flurry of colors and activities. Discuss with your youths, "If we were all the same, what would you miss?"

2. Help your youths learn not just to tolerate differences, but to enjoy them. Expose yourself and them to music, worship, food, literature, clothes, and other aspects of many cultures. By giving them a pleasant experience with others in the safety of your family life, you are expanding their ability to love rather than fear.

3. Kathleen and James McGinnis give the following ideas for families working to combat racism:[7]

a. Inform yourself about racism, past and present. Discuss with your youths.

b. Celebrate racial justice heroes and holidays.

c. Never use or allow racially derogatory terms. Eliminate stereotypes from your thinking.

d. Check TV programming.

e. Involve yourself in community projects and stand with the victims.

4. Years ago UNICEF produced a poster showing how

"interdependent" the world is, by explaining how products from many countries together make up a candy bar. UNICEF thought of materials from ten different countries which together were necessary to create one chocolate bar. Examine some chocolate bars with your youths. How many different countries contributed products? [8] Point out to your youths the country of origin of other foods and articles in your home.

PART B

Story: Jesus came, died, and was raised to bring together Jews and Gentiles.

Faith Focus: Jesus came to heal our relationships with each other as well as with God.

Notes to Parents

1. "Peter Discovers God's Global Community" is the biblical drama that should be read *before* this section (see Contents for "Biblical Dramas").

2. Whom do you tend to call "unclean"? Can you tell a story of God correcting how you thought about others, like he corrected Peter? A time when the globe-surrounding love of God amazed you?

Youth-Adult Reading

Adult: Last time we talked about how people are the same and different.

Youth: And that Jesus helps us not to be afraid of people who are different from us.

Adult: But many of Jesus' fellow Jews, even those who had lived with him, missed this message. They continued to think of Gentiles, the uncircumcised, as not good

enough to be God's people. But Peter had a most surprising dream (Acts 10).

Youth: Is that the one with the sheet that descended from
heaven?

Adult: Yes. Jews had been taught that some animals were
clean and fine for eating and some were unclean and
not fit to eat.

Youth: Cows and chickens were okay to eat but not rabbits
and pigs?

Adult: Right. Those rules are based on the Old Testament. In
the same way, they thought some people could worship God and be their friends, but that others could
not.

Youth: But then Peter went to visit some Gentiles.

**People who develop the habit of
thinking of themselves as world
citizens are fulfilling the first
requirement of sanity in our time.**

—Norman Cousins [9]

Adult: When we actually talk to people different from us and
visit their homes, we are sometimes surprised. *(If
you've had such a conversation, describe the experience.)* Peter found that, not only were these Gentiles
God-fearing, but that the Holy Spirit had been given
to them also. Let's read from Acts.

Youth: "Then Peter began to speak to them: 'I truly understand that God shows no partiality,

Adult: " 'But in every nation anyone who fears him and does
what is right is acceptable to him.

Youth: " 'You know the message he sent to the people of Isra-

el, preaching peace by Jesus Christ —he is Lord of all' " (Acts 10:34-36).

Adult: So Peter had a clear illustration that Jesus' message was for all peoples.

Youth: But we're talking about why we don't go to war! What is the connection?

Adult: Jesus came to remove the fear and the hostility between us that creates war. In Ephesians, Paul also says Jesus came to bring together Jews and Gentiles and make peace between them and with God.

Youth: "But now in Christ Jesus you who once were far off have been brought near by the blood of Christ" (Ephesians 2:13).

Adult: The "you" is the Gentiles. Remember, the Jews considered the uncircumcised Gentiles far from God. This made the Jews call the Gentiles enemies.

Youth: "For [Jesus] is our peace; in his flesh he has made both groups into one and has broken down the dividing wall, that is, the hostility between us.

Adult: "He has abolished the law with its commandments and ordinances, that he might create in himself one new humanity in place of the two, thus making peace, and might reconcile both groups to God in one body through the cross, thus putting to death that hostility through it.

Youth: "So he came and proclaimed peace to you who were far off and peace to those who were near; for through him both of us have access in one Spirit to the Father" (Ephesians 2:14-18).

Adult: That complicated language means that when Jesus died on the cross, he made peace between the Gentiles and the Jews.[10] This passage also says that people need each other to be saved.

Youth: Being saved is not just between me and God?

Adult: No. God cares about how we treat each other. An important reason Jesus came was to make peace between peoples.

Youth: So Jesus also died and was raised to make peace between enemies.

Adult: Right. Too often, we say Jesus just came to make peace between us and God. But at the same time, Jesus was making peace between us and our enemies.

Youth: A double peace! Peace with God is united to peace with others and oneself. So if I go to war and kill an enemy. . . .

Adult: Why don't you read the passage in Matthew where Jesus talks about offering gifts to God?

Youth: "So when you are offering your gift at the altar, if you remember that your brother or sister has something against you, leave your gift there before the altar and go; first be reconciled to your brother or sister, and then come and offer your gift" (Matthew 5:23-24).

Adult: Jesus is saying that you can't worship God when there is a problem between you and another person. For us to be forgiven and loved, we must learn to forgive and love others.

Youth: That makes how we treat enemies important to our relationship with God.

Adult: We just can't kill people and stay right with God.

Youth: That's an important reason for not going to war.

Adult: Earlier we mentioned another reason, when we talked about how God created everyone with different noses.

Youth: What does the shape of noses have to do with war?

Adult: The idea that God created us all is another reason we can't kill others. Even if another person doesn't know God, God still created that person.

Youth: I don't think I'd want to kill a person God made. I don't want to wipe out God's handiwork!

Adult: When people are different from us and worship other gods or seem evil, we must still remember that God made those people.

Youth: And that Jesus came, died, and was raised to save them.

Adult: As well as save us. Jesus came to make a new people, to join peoples together who once were enemies.

Youth: I think what we are saying is that people all over the world are our sisters and brothers in Christ.

Adult: And if you add that to the memory verse—

Youth: The verse said we are to witness to Jesus all over the world. Our job is to tell others about Jesus. We can't do that if we are having war with them.

Adult: So two major reasons we don't go to war are that. . . .

Youth: *(May respond.)*

Adult: Let's pray together the "World Peace Prayer." [11]

All: **Lead me from death to life,**
from falsehood to truth.
Lead me from despair to hope,
from fear to trust.
Lead me from hate to love,
from war to peace.
Let peace fill our heart, our world, our universe.
Amen.

Notes to Parents

1. The New Testament teaching that the atonement, Jesus' blood shed on the cross for us, restores horizontal relation-

ships between people as well as the vertical one between us and God is central to the Mennonite peace position.

2. Like some early Anabaptists, Quakers believe there is "that of God" in each of us. How can you develop the ability in yourself and your youths to listen for God's voice through those you meet?

3. The World Peace Prayer asks God to lead us from negatives to positives. Can you explain to your youths how God has done this for you?

4. Ways to open your family to other cultures abound. Consider "adopting" a student from another country who is attending a local university. Contact neighboring colleges and universities and ask about a host family program for international students. Or, to host a guest during Christmas vacation, contact Christmas International House, PO Box 764, Tucker, GA 30085-9764 (404 938-4291). Students choose between 44 locations in the USA and know they will be visiting a Christian family over the holidays.

Historic Peacemaker

People all over the world have learned love from Jesus. One of these disciples is Simon Kimbangu, who lived in what is now the African country of Zaire. He and the church he founded loved their enemies.

❧ ❧ ❧

Punished for Nothing

Marian Hostetler[12]

Simon Kimbangu was in prison for life. The colonial government of the Belgian Congo had pronounced this sentence on him in 1921. The rulers were afraid of this peaceful prophet of God because thousands of people were flocking to hear his teaching. One of his fellow prisoners, Majewa Apollo, told this story about Kimbangu. At the time of the story, Kimbangu had already been in prison for 25 years.

At the end of one of the long prison buildings were special cells. They were for prisoners who were receiving extra punishment. Some of these had rebelled against the government. Some were mentally ill from their suffering. Some had become like children.

However, one of the prisoners in these cells was different from all the others. His name was Simon Kimbangu.

I learned to know him because I worked in the prison kitchen and took those prisoners their food. Kimbangu's cell was one and one-third meters by two meters. Kimbangu had a cement platform to sleep on, a reed mat on the floor, and two prison blankets.

Kimbangu was a heavy man of medium height. His face was old and wrinkled, his head partly bald with graying hair.

How was he different from us other prisoners? He would take no part in our jealousies and our hatred, no part in our efforts to harm each other. When he wasn't locked up, he would go out each morning to greet each prisoner and shake his hand. When the others persecuted him, he remained calm and peaceful, showing no anger. We could not understand him, but we respected him. We never admitted it, but we knew that his attitude and actions lessened the poisonous feelings in our hearts.

Sometimes he would not eat the food I brought him, and once the prison director beat him for this. The meal following that, he ate his stew, but not the piece of meat in it.

The next day, I saw why. When the 200 prisoners who had been taken out to work in the early morning were being returned in the late afternoon, Kimbangu stood by his cell door. As each one walked by, he gave them a tiny piece of his meat.

Because he had shared his meat, the prison director sent

the guards to take Kimbangu to the torture cell. We knew what happened when the guards took a prisoner there. The guards usually came back carrying the prisoner's body. This time the guards came back alone.

After three days, we saw the guards leading Kimbangu back to his own cell. He went and shook hands with each guard, thanking them! He shook hands with all the prisoners and greeted each of us. Then he went to the prison director's office and greeted him as well!

I could not understand this man! I would threaten someone with death to get a larger piece of meat. He gave his away to others! I did many wrong things, and when I was punished, I planned my revenge. He was punished for nothing and showed only good will to those who did it!

This contact with Kimbangu led to Majewa Apollo's conversion. Five years later, after 30 years in prison, Simon Kimbangu died. The church which had begun from his teaching before his imprisonment is now called the Church of Jesus Christ on Earth by Simon Kimbangu. It has continued to follow—as its leader did—Christ's way of love and peace. Here are two examples.

After Kimbangu's death, the government continued persecuting the church. In the early 1950s it uprooted 37,000 Kimbanguist families from their homes and sent them to other parts of the country. However, the church continued to grow—and so did persecution of it.

Finally in 1956, some 600 leading Kimbanguist residents of Kinshasa wrote a letter to the Belgian governor general. "We are suffering so much. Wherever we meet for prayer, we are arrested by your soldiers," they said. "In order not to burden the police with added work, we shall all gather unarmed in the stadium where you can arrest us all at once or massacre us."

While the letter was being delivered, thousands of Kimbanguists left their jobs and gathered peacefully at the stadium for arrest or death. The governor general was stunned.

He could not grant them official recognition, but he did grant them "toleration," and they were neither arrested nor killed.

In 1964 after the independent Congo had become Zaire, the government army came in Kisangani to fight the Simba rebels. The Kimbanguist Christians of that place had a simple church made of posts stuck in the ground with a palm branch roof. As the fighting came closer and closer, 170 of the Kimbanguists gathered in their palm branch church to pray. Though they had refused to participate in any fighting, they now feared for their lives.

As the Simba rebels began to flee from the government army, they threw grenades and shot at the praying people. Some of the government soldiers were flying overhead in an army plane. When they saw the praying crowd, they thought it was a group of rebels and began firing on them, too.

What could the Christians do? They stayed there, shot at from every side. They were ready to die, but not willing to kill. They continued to pray.

At last a Belgian officer and some government soldiers arrived and demanded, "What are you doing there?"

"We are praying," they answered.

"Yes. Praying for the rebels, no doubt," sneered the officer.

"We're praying for all God's children and for peace," said the pastor, showing his Bible. The officer took it, looked at it, put it in his pocket, and ordered his men to go on their way.

During this whole time, no one was even wounded. The Kimbanguists knew God had protected them.

❧   ❧   ❧

Contemporary Peacemaker

Many of the people who answer God's call to follow the path of peace discover that their journey leads them overseas. John Paul Lederach is a Mennonite Central Committee (MCC) worker with a special gift and training in mediation.

When John Paul mediates, he helps two disagreeing groups find ways to get along with each other. He has helped Native Americans cope with their conflicts in both Nicaragua and Canada. He has also advised a group of Somalians working to bring peace to their country. Sometimes this put him and his family in dangerous situations as he lived out Jesus' call. Read this interview with John Paul, and/or interview a local peacemaker (see questions on page 22):

When I was little, I fought all the time with my brother. We had the typical ongoing sibling rivalry. When we were traveling, it almost drove our parents nuts. Sometimes to get us to stop fighting, they would put us out on the road, drive ahead a half mile, and make us walk to the car. Learning to handle fighting among kids is good for making peacemakers!

Once my mom tried a new technique to deal with our fighting. She had me and my brother sit beside each other on chairs and look at an artist's depiction of Joseph's brothers making ugly faces at him because they were jealous of his coat.

The image of doing good to someone who does bad to you comes to me from way back. Jesus taught us to love our enemies and help them like Dirk Willems rescued his enemy who broke through the ice (the "Historic Peacemaker" story in chapter 2). I also remember family stories. My grandparents owned a house they rented out. The renters trashed it. They even chopped up the cupboards and used them for kindling. My grandparents' choice not to take the renters to court taught me what to do about people who have treated me badly.

When I was in fifth grade and lived in Goshen, Indiana, two of my friends got into a huge fight. They were beating each other up badly. I jumped in the middle, pushed them apart, and yelled at both of them. I have some memories of times like that—but I still fought with my brother!

When Martin Luther King, Jr., was killed in 1968, riots broke out in Winston-Salem, North Carolina, where we lived. I was in seventh grade. The whole school system was closed down for a day or two. When we came back, my first class was social studies, and every morning it started with a review of the news. My classmates stood up and bad-mouthed Martin Luther King. They said his death was long overdue. I stood up and said I thought he was a great leader and had done a lot for his people in a way that respected other people's lives. I clearly remember that while I was still speaking, a classmate sitting beside me blurted out, "What are you, a nigger lover?" The teacher didn't reprimand him or anything. I sat down in great embarrassment. It was the first time I understood that what *we* believed was so different from what my peers believed. That marked me.

Currently, there are thirty-five wars in the world. In many of those places, we have people of our own church, Mennonites, who are caught. Daily they have to figure out how to respond to the fact that people from within their own country are divided, hate each other, and are actively trying to kill each other. I feel called of God to try to resolve some of those situations and find ways that wars can end and people can move on to issues like jobs, housing, education, and health care. When I mediate, I am trying to find ways to get people to move away from talking to each other through the end of the gun, and move to talking to each other with words.

Then I help them find a solution with which everyone can agree.

In both Nicaragua and Somalia, I got caught in circumstances that were complicated and risky. In Nicaragua we were working between the Sandinista government and Indians who lived on the east coast. Those of us on the mediation team accompanied a group of people on their way to a meeting, and a full-blown riot broke out. We were caught in the middle, and it was exciting to deal with getting stoned and beat up!

Several years ago in Somalia, before the United Nations had international troops there, I went to Mogadishu to meet with several leaders and talk about the peace process. A guide escorted me everywhere I went. We traveled with two sixteen-year-olds who pointed machine guns out of various windows of the car. Apparently, if we didn't have those, we'd have been shot at. But I felt odd being accompanied by these young people. I asked one of the kids when he last was in school. It turned out that he couldn't read or write, but he was handling a sophisticated antitank piece of weaponry. (His reply is available on a poster from MCC.)

If you and your friends want personally to hear some of my exciting stories about mediating around the world, contact me at Eastern Mennonite College, 1200 Park Road, Harrisonburg, VA 22801-2462; phone 703 432-4450.

Let love be genuine;
hate what is evil,
hold fast to what is good;
love one another
with mutual affection;
outdo one another
in showing honor.

Romans 12:9-10

Session 6

We Make Peace

Summary: We don't go to war because we choose to follow Jesus' way of peace and spread more love and justice in the world.

Memory Verse: *Let us love, not in word or speech, but in truth and action* (1 John 3:18).

Bible Texts Behind Session 6

Luke 4:18-19   James 2:18
Romans 12:9-21   1 Peter 3:11
Romans 14:19   1 John 3:18
1 Thessalonians 5:13

PART A

Story: Deciding to be a peacemaker and to follow Jesus will change your life.

Faith Focus: Because Jesus loves us, we want to give love to others by making more peace in the world.

143

I worked on the hacienda over there, and I would have to feed the dogs bowls of meat or bowls of milk every morning, and I could never put those on the table for my own children. When my children were ill, they died with a nod of sympathy from the landlord. But when the dogs were ill, I took them to the veterinarian in Suchitoto.

You will never understand violence or nonviolence until you understand the violence to the spirit that happens from watching your children die of malnutrition.

—*A peasant in El Salvador*[1]

Word List

injustice   Something unfair. It is an *injustice* that some people have too much to eat and waste food while other people are dying from hunger.

Kids know, better than grownups, what we do is more important than what we say.

—*Pete Seeger*[2]

Notes to Parents:

1. This session begins with a review of the five previous sessions. Think back over your times together. What has gone well? What do you want to continue working on? What concepts do you yourself want to explore further?

2. Can you think of how your life has changed since you decided to follow Jesus' way of peace? Be ready to tell your youth.

3. How do you deal with the injustice you see? Does it overwhelm you, or are you able to act to overcome some of it?

4. This session provides time for you to introduce a family project that brings more justice to the world. For ideas, see appendix 3.

Youth-Adult Conversation

Adult: We have almost completed our study. Before we discuss how being a peacemaker is more than not going to war, let's review what we've learned. What do you remember from the first session?

Youth: *(May respond.)*

Adult: *(Add comments.)* Jesus chose not to seek revenge or make war, but rather to heal and help. And if we choose to follow Jesus, we will imitate how he lived. Then we talked about loving our enemies. What sticks in your mind about the second session?

Youth: *(May respond.)* I claimed it was difficult to love enemies, and you said I needed to depend on Jesus to help. But I still don't know if I could help someone trying to kill me, like Dirk Willems did.

Adult: I don't know if I could either. But when I hear the stories of those who loved enemies and learn more about Jesus and about God's way of peace, I find ideas about how to try. What do you remember about the third session, on trusting God first?

Youth: *(May respond.)* We talked about those who obeyed

God rather than the government and how we need to
follow the leading of the Holy Spirit, like Peter did.

Adult: And then in the fourth session, we looked at your
friend David!

Youth: *(May respond.)* I never heard the part before about
God refusing to let David build the temple because he
had killed people. That helped me understand how serious God is about a way of peace.

Adult: In session 5 we talked about God being Lord of all.

Youth: And about others around the world being our sisters
and brothers.

Adult: What other ideas would you like to discuss?

Youth: *(May respond.)*

Adult: How many of the memory verses can you say without
peeking?

Youth: *(May respond.)* And which ones can you say?

Adult: *(May respond.)* So we've explored lots of reasons why
Christians don't go to war. But being a peacemaker is
more than not being a soldier.

> **It is crucial that we begin to
> understand peace to mean, not only an
> end to war, but an end to all the ways
> we do violence to ourselves, each
> other, the animals, the earth.**
>
> —*Pam McAllister*[3]

Youth: You mean that to follow Jesus' way of peace, I do more
than choose *not* to enlist in the military?

Adult: That's right. When you decide to follow Jesus and
make more love and justice in the world, it will

change your life. Can you think of ways it will change
how you live?

Youth: *(May respond.)*

Adult: *(Explain a way it has changed your own life.)* Jesus
taught us to love, and that will touch all of our
lives—how we treat our friends and family as well as
our enemies, what career we choose, how we spend
our money, and what we do with our time.

Youth: That sounds like the memory verse,

All: **"Let us love, not in word or speech, but in truth and
action"** (1 John 3:18).

Adult: We must do more than say no to war. We must proclaim YES! to life with Jesus.

Youth: That's fancy talk. What do you mean?

Adult: Right now, there is no draft and no war. So it's easy to
sit here and say war is against God's will, so we won't
take part. "Being a pacifist between wars is as easy as
being a vegetarian between meals."[4]

Youth: Like the memory verse, that's loving in word. How do
we love in truth and action? How do we heal and
help?

Adult: First let's think about where healing and helping are
needed. Where do you see injustice in the world?

Youth: *(May respond.)*

Adult: Before we can help make justice, we have to see and
feel the injustice. How do you feel when you see hungry children or a home destroyed by war?

Youth: *(May respond.)*
Adult: *(Share how you feel.)* What I want to feel is hope.
Youth: How can you look at such horrible, unfair things and feel hope?
Adult: Usually I can't. But someone said that "Hope has two daughters, Anger and Courage: Anger that things are not what they ought to be, and Courage to make them what they must be. This is the hope of the peacemaker."[5]
Youth: I'm good at the anger.
Adult: Me too. Sometimes I get so angry inside that I don't have any room left for the courage.
Youth: But I need courage to work for justice!
Adult: Right. The anger helps me see the injustice, the courage helps me change it. How might our family heal and help in the places of injustice you mentioned?
Youth: *(May respond.)*
Adult: *(Add your ideas. You may want to go on here and discuss a family project or save that for the next session.)* Many Christians have chosen to be missionaries or work with service and relief agencies overseas. Many have also done voluntary service here in the United States and Canada and helped clean up after disasters.
Youth: Has anyone we know done those things?
Adult: *(May respond.)* But let's remember why we do those things.
Youth: Because we're angry at injustice!
Adult: We have to have more than anger, and even more than courage. All of our actions must be a response to the love which Jesus shows us and that we want to pass on to others.
Youth: That might change how I work against injustice.
Adult: It might. Let's pray.
All: **Lord Jesus, fill us with your love. Help us to see you in people who suffer injustice. Give us hope, so we are**

angry at the hurts of the world. Give us courage to help change and heal these aches. Guide our feet on the path to your peace. Amen.

Notes to Parents

Sometimes when we are confronted with the injustice of the world, we wonder what difference we could possibly make. But it is important that we act.

1. If we show God's love to just one person, it makes an enormous difference in that person's life.

2. Christ calls us to faithfulness. We witness to the faith and hope Christ gave us by acting to end the violence and bring wholeness to the world. See James 2:18.

3. Acts of justice done in Jesus' name free us from our own fears of powerlessness. We find "true security and love."

4. "Miracles are what happen when God's justice and righteousness are present."[6]

PART B

Story: Jesus does not command us to overcome evil with evil, but to overcome evil with good.

Faith Focus: True faith in Jesus will make us willing to risk everything to follow Jesus' call to make peace.

Note to Parents

1. This is your last conversation together with your junior youth in this series. How will you celebrate completing the study? How will you affirm your youths and tell them how much you've enjoyed learning along with them?

2. Who are the peacemakers who inspire you and your family? Try not to think only of people like Mother Teresa, but also about folks from your church and neighborhood that your youths know.

Youth-Adult Conversation

Adult: Last time we talked about our actions being a response to the love Jesus has shown us. Let's repeat the memory verse.

All: **"Let us love, not in word or speech, but in truth and action"** (1 John 3:18).

Youth: We said we pass love on to others because Jesus first loved us.

Adult: And what does this love do when it sees injustice?

Youth: *(May respond.)* But just how do we go about healing and helping?

Adult: For answers, let's start by looking at Romans.

Youth: "Let love be genuine; hate what is evil, hold fast to what is good; love one another with mutual affection; outdo one another in showing honor.

Adult: "Do not lag in zeal, be ardent in spirit, serve the Lord. Rejoice in hope, be patient in suffering, persevere in prayer. Contribute to the needs of the saints; extend hospitality to strangers.

Youth: "Bless those who persecute you; bless and do not curse them. Rejoice with those who rejoice, weep with those who weep.

Adult: "Live in harmony with one another; do not be haughty, but associate with the lowly; do not claim to be wiser than you are.

Youth: "Do not repay anyone evil for evil, but take thought for what is noble in the sight of all.

Adult: "If it is possible, so far as it depends on you, live peaceably with all. Beloved, never avenge yourselves, but leave room for the wrath of God; for it is written, 'Vengeance is mine, I will repay, says the Lord.'

Youth: "No, 'if your enemies are hungry, feed them; if they are thirsty, give them something to drink; for by doing this you will heap burning coals on their heads.' Do not be overcome by evil, but overcome evil with good" (Romans 12:9-21).

Adult: After our talk about the vision of peace in the Old Testament, I find it interesting that the part about feeding enemies is from Proverbs.

Youth: What does that last part mean, "Do not be overcome by evil, but overcome evil with good"?

Adult: What do you think it means?

Youth: *(May respond.)*

Adult: Perhaps it means that if someone is mean to us and we are mean back, we have given in to evil. Evil has won. But if someone is mean to us and we are able to respond with the love of Jesus, we have overcome evil. Good has won.

Youth: But that doesn't always work! If I'm nice to someone who is mean, I might just get clobbered again!

Adult: That is a real possibility. A difficult thing to understand about Jesus' call to the way of peace is that there is no guarantee that we will be successful, at least in the world's eyes.

Youth: A little more explanation, please.

Adult: Well, to the world, Jesus' life looks like a failure. Let's think about what the world tells us is the good life. What does the world tell us to want?

Youth: *(May respond.)*

Adult: Now, when the world looked at Jesus, did he seem successful?

Youth: *(May respond.)*

Adult: He started a movement and had a parade with lots of people singing his praises.

Youth: That's when people thought he was successful.

Adult: But then, only a week later, he was hung as a common criminal, and his disciples ran away from him. He died on a cross with little wealth to his name and only a few faithful friends.

Youth: But several days later he was raised from the dead, and now the whole world knows about Jesus!

Adult: Well, at least much of the world. But to the people living just then, Jesus and the way of peace did not seem at all successful. And to many people today, the idea of suffering to show love is just plain stupid.

Youth: So you're saying that sometimes the way of peace looks like it doesn't work today also?

Adult: Some people are willing to die in order to follow Jesus. That doesn't look successful.

Youth: That's like Dirk Willems. But his courage influenced many others to turn to the way of peace! That's success!

Adult: In a manner of speaking. But even that doesn't always happen. The point is to remember that we are called to be faithful to Jesus' way, which may not always seem effective to the world. Do you understand the difference?

Youth: *(May respond.)* What else does a peacemaker do to love in truth and action?

Adult: Those verses from Romans have other ideas. What do you see?

Youth: *(May respond.)*

Adult: Keep going! There's more!

Youth: *(May respond.)*

Adult: So peacemakers love, rejoice, pray, are kind to strangers, and feed the hungry. Peacemakers act to create more peace in the world.

Youth: We said before that peace in the Old Testament is love and justice together.

Adult: And just what is justice?

Youth: *(May respond.)*

Adult: So part of the work of the peacemaker is to help make happen what you just explained.

Youth: I don't think I can do all that alone.

Adult: Right again! I think that is the reason Jesus created a movement, which we now call the church. Jesus didn't call just one person to follow him, but twelve disciples and countless others who walked with him day by day.

Youth: And these people worked to make more justice?

Adult: Yes, they did, by healing people and teaching others how to forgive and love. They didn't all agree how to do it, and they had different ways of understanding Jesus' life and call, but the faithful kept learning and growing.

Youth: The early church didn't always agree, did it?

Adult: No! There were terrible arguments, some of them recorded in Acts, about how the work of Jesus should be done.[7]

Youth: Maybe that's why there are so many verses in the Bible about learning to live together in peace and love!

Adult: Yes, Paul emphasizes that.[8] And today, people continue to have different ideas about how to help bring more peace and justice.

Youth: So there are different kinds of peacemakers?
Adult: Yes. Who are some peacemakers you know about?
Youth: *(May respond.)*
Adult: *(Mention one of your favorite peacemakers.)* Some are beginners in making peace, and others have lived this way for years. Some serve in soup kitchens, some tutor students, and—what more can you think of?
Youth: *(May respond.)* Some write letters to their congress-people, some volunteer to go overseas.

It isn't enough to talk about peace. One must believe in it. And it isn't enough to believe in it. One must work at it.

—Eleanor Roosevelt[9]

Adult: Some serve in Christian Peacemaker Teams, some take part in nonviolent demonstrations. *(Add others.)*
Youth: And some learn, like we are with this study.
Adult: *All* learn and *all* grow. All the faithful continue searching for the next step they need to take to follow Jesus' way of peace. Have you thought of more ways our family can make love and justice in the world?
Youth: *(May respond.)*
Adult: *(You may outline a plan for a family project if you didn't previously.)* So, even as we finish this study, we will continue to learn and to grow and to search for ways for our family to make peace and justice in this world.
Youth: You make it sound like we'll never get done!
Adult: We won't, but we won't be bored. Trust that working to bring God's peace and justice to our world will be exciting and fascinating.

As you come to know the seriousness of our situation—the war, the racism, the poverty in the world—you come to realize it is not going to be changed just by words or demonstrations. It's a question of risking your life. It's a question of living your life in drastically different ways.

—Dorothy Day[10]

Youth: I'm not sure I'm ready for the kinds of excitement we've read and heard about! What if this peacemaking is just too hard?

Adult: That's a good question. It is a great risk to decide to follow Jesus and be a peacemaker. We have to have faith that if we let go of what the world calls success and cling instead to Jesus, we will find a new life, like Jesus promised.

Youth: What do I need to have faith in?

Adult: "We need to believe
    that love and life are stronger than death,
    that truth will prevail over lies,
    that Jesus lives and we will too if we are willing
    to lose our lives in following him."[11]

Youth: That's a mouthful! What if I make mistakes?

Adult: We may fail, but we'll continue, with God's grace and goodness. But think also about the joy! We are learning to love and do justice. We're taking part in God's miracles! That's something to celebrate!

Youth: Celebrate? With cake and ice cream and balloons?

Adult: Sometimes. But the celebration of justice and love
will also include "proclaiming release to the captives,
recovery of sight to the blind, letting the oppressed go
free, and proclaiming the year of the Lord's favor"
(Luke 4:18-19, paraphrased).

Youth: That sounds like quite a celebration! I want to be
there!

Adult: Great! I'm glad we'll be there together. We've almost
completed these conversations. Is there anything further you'd like to ask?

Youth: *(May respond.)*

Adult: *(Share your feelings about having this time together.
Show affirmation!)* To end, let's read from 1 Peter.

Youth: "Seek peace and pursue it" (1 Peter 3:11b).

Adult: Those verbs *seek* and *pursue* are action words. Making
peace and doing justice are *actions*. Let's pray an action prayer, written by St. Francis of Assisi, which has
been popular with peacemakers through the years.[12]

All: **Lord,**
> **make me an instrument of thy peace.**
Where there is hatred, let me sow love;
> **where there is injury, pardon;**
> **where there is doubt, faith;**
> **where there is despair, hope;**
> **where there is darkness, light;**
> **where there is sadness, joy;**
O divine Master,
> **grant that I may not so much seek**
>> **to be consoled, as to console;**
>> **to be understood, as to understand;**
>> **to be loved, as to love.**
For it is in giving that we receive;
> **it is in pardoning that we are pardoned;**
> **it is in dying that we are born to eternal life.**
>> **Amen.**

Notes to Parents

1. If your youths enjoy drawing, have them make a mural depicting the actions of Romans 12:9-21. Invite visitors to your home to add to it.

2. Perhaps, like me, you get "plumb tuckered out" when faced with the injustice of the world. We need to both accept and test our limits, as veteran peacemaker and educator, James McGinnis, explains in four points:

a. *Pray.* Pray that you will be aware of Jesus working in the world. Pray for others working for justice and peace. Pray that God will show you what to do.

b. *Set priorities.* You just can't do it all. (Thank goodness! We already have a Savior.) Choose the issues you want to concentrate on and do as good a job on them as you can.

c. *Encourage others.* Others have taken on the issues you can't. Look for ways to encourage them.

d. *Acknowledge your sinfulness.* When you don't respond to injustice because of your own selfishness, confess that. "Ask for forgiveness, and remember how Jesus accepted his disciples that 'first day back on the job' after they deserted him in his agony and death. 'Peace be with you.' "[13]

3. Every day we are confronted with the risk of accepting Jesus and truly believing he will do what he promises he will do. What have you risked? What is God inviting you to risk further? "Peacemaking is finally a way of life, removing barriers that separate who we are from whom we can become, so that we can become reconciled with God, ourselves, those around us, the earth, and humankind."[14] God be with you on that journey.

Historic Peacemaker

In the early 1950s, Elizabeth Hershberger Bauman collected stories based on verses from Romans 12:20-21.

"If your enemies are hungry, feed them; if they are thirsty, give them something to drink; for by doing this you will heap coals of fire on their heads." Do not be overcome by evil, but overcome evil with good. (NRSV/KJV)

She entitled the book *Coals of Fire.* Her stories have shaped generations of Christians who wanted to know whether it really is possible to overcome evil with good. These extraordinary examples of God's love making good triumph over evil have encouraged many to trust Jesus and try the humanly impossible. The guiding verse for "Mystery of the Thatch" is Matthew 5:44 (KJV): "Do good to them that hate you."

ろ   ろ   ろ

The Mystery of the Thatch

Elizabeth Hershberger Bauman [15]

If Preacher Peter had been awake, he would have heard their quick footsteps as the shadowy figures of the young men made their way down the cobblestone street of the little village in the Emmenthal, Switzerland.

Each step brought the young men closer and closer to the darkened home of the old Mennonite minister and his wife. Life for them had been very difficult, for they lived in the eighteenth century when Mennonites were still being persecuted in Switzerland.

"Now we will see what kind of a man he is," muttered one of the young men. "Maybe he won't be so loving after our visit tonight!" he laughed.

"That is the house," whispered another as they slackened their pace. Cautiously they approached the darkened dwelling while their eyes searched the darkness.

"No one is stirring. Let us do our job well."

The men quickly lifted themselves to the roof and soon the

muffled sound of falling thatch blended in with other night sounds. They worked quickly lest someone should surprise them in their treachery.

Inside Peter stirred in his sleep. The strange sounds continued and Peter sat up in his bed.

"Something is not right," thought Peter. "There are noises on the roof."

Carefully he made his way across the bedroom floor,

through the darkened room, and reaching the outside doorway he quietly opened the latch. Peering cautiously into the night he could make out the figures of several men busily at work.

"What can this mean!" he gasped, as he stared in amazement. "Destroying my thatch!"

Slowly the meaning of their actions became clear to him. He knew that many people in the Emmenthal did not understand why he and his people believed it was wrong to go to war. When they had been threatened with imprisonment and death, Peter and his friends would simply say, "We would rather die the bitterest death than disobey God."

"Now they have come to molest me again," thought Peter.

Raising his eyes heavenward, Peter prayed to God to help him do what was right. Then turning, he walked quickly into the little house.

"Mother," he called, "workmen have come to us; you had better prepare a meal."

The strange happenings of the past few minutes had startled his wife, but now she understood. Soon she was busily at work in the little kitchen. And before long a meal was waiting on the neatly spread table.

Opening the door once more, the aged minister called to the boys on the roof, "You have worked long and hard. Surely you are hungry. Now come in to us and eat."

Hesitatingly they came into the room and stood awkwardly around the table where the lighted tapers gave the room a friendly glow. Peter urged them to be seated and finally they found their places where they sat uncomfortably, staring at their plates.

Peter bowed his head and folded his hands while the guests sat in silence. Then in his kindly voice, Peter prayed earnestly and fervently and lovingly for the guests and for his family. When the last words of the kindly prayer were spoken, the young men raised faces flushed with shame. The food was passed and found its way onto their plates, but it seemed they could not eat. Each sat silent before his well-filled plate.

Suddenly, as if by signal, the men pushed back their chairs and quickly disappeared through the door which they had entered moments before. Once again there were footsteps on the roof, and the shuffle of thatch could be heard. But this time it was not the sound of falling thatch. They were putting it back on the roof! Then, if Preacher Peter were listening (and I think he was), he would have heard the running footsteps of his guests as they disappeared down the cobblestone street and into the night.

***

Contemporary Peacemaker

Lois Kenagy, who lives in Oregon, chose the career of being a volunteer peacemaker. She has served both her community and the Mennonite Church. Read this interview with Lois, and/or interview a local peacemaker (see questions on page 22):

The Golden Rule (Matthew 7:12) guided our family as I was growing up. We were poor, but there were many people around us poorer than we were. We always had enough to eat and clothes to wear, even if some clothing came from relatives. But some of these poor people would come to visit us over mealtime. I would be annoyed, and I would say, "Mother, you know they just come to visit us now at dinnertime." Mother would reply, "Lois, go, put another plate down. Don't complain. We want to share." My mother's example helped shape my life. She was always sharing, always willing to think how others felt.

When I learned history and the story of Abraham Lincoln, I wondered whether he could go to heaven. I knew we were not to go to war. I asked my mother if Lincoln could go to heaven after he had led the Civil War. My mother responded, "God is the judge. I don't have to judge other people." So I learned that I was to do what I knew God was calling me to do without being judgmental of other people who were trying to do what they thought was right.

As a young adult, I worked in Europe after World War II. I saw victims of war and was impressed by the tragedy that war and injustice brought for people. An adult friend helped me see things from the viewpoint of others outside the United States and understand how our government was acting toward them. That friend helped me see the need for Christians to talk to our government about things the government is doing wrong.

During the Vietnam War, I saw that our young Mennonite men were easily obtaining their CO (conscientious objector) classification. However, many other young men who also believed war was wrong were being thrown into jail, or had to leave the country, or were sent to the army, where they didn't want to be. That greatly affected me. So I began to do draft counseling for non-Mennonite people, those who couldn't say, "My church teaches me war is wrong," but had to explain for themselves what they believed. That began my peace work.

Right now, I am concerned about people in our own church communities who say they are doing God's will but are being hateful toward other groups of people. Sometimes those who follow Jesus' way don't agree, and we have to make peace among ourselves. I am working at helping people love and respect each other in our own communities.

Christians are to do what God calls them to do. Sometimes doing what is right leads to suffering and death, but we do the best we can, trying to find the Jesus way. Peacemaking was the calling given to me, the gifts God gave me, and the work that needed to be done. We have to look at the needs in our world, the needs in our communities, discover what we can do about them. We try to use the Golden Rule, to see things from the other's point of view. Being open to other people's pain can lead to suffering and joy. The pilgrimage of following Jesus is exciting. We don't know where it will lead us!

I live on a family farm in Oregon. If you live nearby, we can talk together about peacemaking. Contact me at 1640 Nebergall Loop NE, Albany, OR 97321; phone 503 928-6834.

> **What I want to bring out is how a pebble cast into a pond causes ripples that spread in all directions. And each one of our thoughts, words, and deeds is like that.**
>
> —Dorothy Day[16]

They shall beat their swords
    into plowshares,
and their spears
    into pruning hooks;
nation shall not lift up sword
    against nation,
neither shall they learn war
    any more....

Micah 4:3

Biblical Dramas

Elisha Makes Peace

Based on 2 Kings 6:8-23
(Use before session 2, part A.)

Characters:

Aramean Officer	*King of Israel*
Elisha	*Narrator*
King of Aram	*Servant of Elisha*

Narrator: Now the king of Aram was at war with Israel. After consulting his officers, he decided where to set up his camp. The man of God, Elisha, then sent word to the king of Israel:

Elisha: Don't go down that way because the Arameans are going down there to set up a camp.

Narrator: So the king of Israel checked on the place Elisha told him about. Time and again Elisha warned the king, so that he was on his guard to avoid the Aramean camps. This enraged the king of Aram, and he was greatly perturbed. He summoned his officers.

King of Aram: (In a demanding voice) Tell me who of us is on the side of the king of Israel? Who tells him where all our camps are? How can we win a war if someone is constantly giving the enemy this important information?

Officer: None of us is doing this, my lord the king. But Elisha, the prophet who is in Israel, tells the king of Israel the very words you speak in your bedroom.

King of Aram: (With authority) Go, find out where he is so I can send men and capture him. This must be stopped!

Narrator: The king's men went and searched and soon reported back.

Officer: He is in Dothan.

King of Aram: Take horses and chariots and a strong force there! Go by night and surround the city. I want Elisha!

Narrator: Early the next morning, the servant of Elisha, the man of God, got up and went outside. He quickly ran back in.

Servant: Elisha! Elisha! Wake up! An army with horses and chariots has surrounded the city! Oh, my lord, what shall we do?

Elisha: Don't be afraid. There are more with us than there are with them. *(Praying)* O Lord, please open his eyes so he may see.

Narrator: Then the Lord opened the servant's eyes and he saw.

Servant: My lord! I see hills full of horses and chariots of fire all around you! But the enemy is also coming fast!

Elisha: *(Praying)* Please strike these enemy soldiers with blindness.

Narrator: So God struck them with blindness, as Elisha had asked.

Elisha: *(Tricking the soldiers of Aram)* Soldiers of the king of Aram! This is not the road and this is not the city you want. Follow me, and I will lead you to the man you are looking for. Did you say his name is Elisha?

Narrator: And Elisha led them to Samaria, where the king of Israel lived, and they entered the city.

Elisha: *(Praying)* Lord, open the eyes of these men so they can see.

Officer: Oh no! How did we get here? We're inside Samaria, home of our terrible enemies! We're dead meat!

King of Israel: My enemies! *(Delighted, begging permission from Elisha)* Shall I kill them, my father? Shall I kill them?

Elisha: Do not kill them. Would you kill men you have captured with your own sword or bow? Set food and water before them so that they may eat and drink, and then let them go back to their master.

Narrator: So the king of Israel prepared a great feast for his enemies. After they had finished eating and drinking, he sent them away, and they returned to the king of Aram. So the bands from Aram stopped raiding Israel's territory.

❧   ❧   ❧

Peter Disobeys

Based on Acts 5:12-42
(Use before session 3, part B.)

Characters:

Angel	*High Priest*	*Peter*
An Apostle	*Gamaliel*	*Sadducee*
An Elder	*Guard (and assistants)*	

High Priest: Have you heard about this fellow Peter? I am amazed at how the people love him! He and the other so-called apostles of this fellow Jesus are all together in Solomon's Portico, a part of the temple.

Sadducee: Jesus? But we killed him. Wasn't that the end of that?

High Priest: I guess not. Every day great numbers of both men and women are being added to those who believe in him. And they think this Peter fellow has the same magic. They even carry out the sick onto the streets, and lay them on cots and mats, in hope that Peter's shadow might fall on some of them as he comes by.

Sadducee: Oh, so that's the huge crowd of people who come from all the towns around Jerusalem. They bring the sick and those tormented by unclean spirits, and he probably pretends to cure them!

High Priest: I can't stand anyone else being so popular! Arrest Peter and all the other apostles. The people will soon forget about these Jesus-lovers when they are locked away in prison.

Sadducee: Excellent idea. Guard! Go arrest Peter and the other apostles. Shut them up in prison so they won't trouble anyone, and so they will be out of our hair.

(In Solomon's Portico)

Guard: Here, now, you strange Jesus-lovers, you're to come with me.

Peter: Where are you taking us?

Guard: We're off to prison, where you won't create such a ruckus.

Peter: But what have we done?

Guard: Quit your mumbling and come along quietly.

(In the jail cell)

Peter: This place isn't even fit for rats. Have you ever seen such dirty water? I didn't know the dark could be so deep.

Apostle: I thought we were doing God's will by preaching and healing. Doesn't our government understand that?

Peter: Just because the high priest is an Israelite, as Jesus and we are, doesn't mean that we see eye to eye.

Remember, the temple leaders got the Romans to crucify Jesus. *(Looking around)* Can you figure out any way to actually sleep here?

Apostle: Why don't you try to sleep first and I'll stop the rats from biting you. Then we can trade off. Good night.

(Later)

Peter: *(Awakened and dazed by brightness)* Where is this light coming from? It's so dazzling and white that I can't bear to look at it! But I can hear the prison doors creaking open.

Angel: Go, stand in the temple and tell the people the message about Jesus and how to live.

Apostle: Come on, Peter! Let's get out of here and go back to the temple. Then we can continue preaching about Jesus and helping the people.

(The next morning)

High Priest: Call together the council and the whole body of the elders of Israel. And bring those troublemakers from prison so we can all hear them.

Sadducee: Yes sir! Guard, quickly bring the prisoners. Let's see if a night in the dungeon brought them to their senses.

(A little while later)

Guard: Sirs, you won't believe this, but we found the prison securely locked and the guards standing at the doors. But when we opened the cell, we found no one inside.

High Priest: But that's impossible! Guard, you can expect a beating or something much worse if you don't soon find those men.

Elder: *(Breathless)* I'm sorry I'm late for your meeting, High Priest. But look, the men whom you put in prison are standing in the temple and teaching the people!

Guard: I'll bring them here on the double, sir!

High Priest: Don't be violent or the people might stone you!

(Later)

Guard: *(Roughly)* Now, you rabble-rousers and escapees, stand here before the council. The High Priest himself has questions for you!

High Priest: (Sternly) We gave you strict orders not to teach in Jesus' name. Yet here you have filled Jerusalem with your teaching, and you are determined to blame us for killing Jesus.

Peter: We must obey God rather than any human authority. The God of our ancestors raised up Jesus, whom you had killed by hanging him on a tree. God exalted him at his right hand as Leader and Savior that he might give repentance to Israel and forgiveness of sins. And we are witnesses to these things, and so is the Holy Spirit whom God has given to those who obey him.

High Priest: (Bellowing in anger) I'll have you killed! Don't you know you're speaking to one of your highest government officials? You'll soon be dead!

Gamaliel: Put the prisoners outside, Guard. I have something to say.

High Priest: We will respect your wishes, Gamaliel, since you are our most important Jewish teacher. Take them out, Guard, but don't let them get away.

Gamaliel: Fellow Israelites, consider carefully what you do to these men. Some time ago Theudas rose up, claiming to be somebody, and about 400 men joined him. But he was killed, and all who followed him were dispersed and disappeared. After him Judas the Galilean rose up at the time of the census and got people to follow him. He also perished, and all who followed him were scattered. So in this case, I tell you, keep away from these men and leave them alone. If this plan or this undertaking is of human origin, it will fail. But if it is of God, you will not be able to overthrow them —in that case you may even be found to be fighting against God!

High Priest: You speak well, Gamaliel. Guard, bring the prisoners back in and beat them so they will better remember our commands.

Guard: Yes sir! You mean the forty lashes minus one, like they gave that Jesus they are always talking about? *(To his assistants)* Bring the prisoners and plenty of whips!

(After the beating)

High Priest: Now listen carefully. You are not to speak in the name of Jesus ever again, or we'll not be easy on you. Understand? You may leave now.

(Outside)

Apostle: Did you hear that, Peter? *Again* they tell us not to preach about Jesus. What will we do? Shouldn't we obey our government?

Peter: First we obey God. And God has called us to teach and proclaim Jesus as the Messiah every day in the temple and from house to house. We will never cease doing what God commands.

✎ ✎ ✎

Israel Begs for a King

Based on 1 Samuel 8
(Use before session 4, part A.)

Characters:

Elder 1 of Israel   *Elder 2 of Israel*
Samuel   *The Lord God*
The people of Israel

Elder 1: Israel should stop having judges! All the nations
around us have kings who tell the people what to do.
We only have a judge to give us God's commands.

Elder 2: I agree! I want us to be like everyone else! Even
though our judges claim to speak for God, this just
isn't working.

Elder 1: Right! Samuel is too old to be of any use, and his sons
are evil. They take bribes and don't make good
decisions. We won't have justice with them as judges.

Elder 2: Let's go, talk to Samuel, and tell him we demand a
king.

(In conversation with Samuel)

Elder 1: Samuel, we need to talk. Maybe it's time Israel
stopped having judges and started having kings.

Samuel: Not have a judge? But that is God's command!

Elder 2: But it's just not working Samuel! You're getting old,
and your sons are neither fair nor just.

Samuel: But how can you ask for a human king to rule you?
Israel has a covenant with God. *God* is our only king.

Elder 1: We're ready to be like other nations, Samuel. We've
waited a long time and given the idea of using judges
a chance. Now we want to have a human king.

Samuel: But we are not like other nations! We have the Lord
for our king! I am not at all pleased with this idea. I'll
talk to God about it.

(Alone, Samuel praying)

Samuel: God, the people are begging for a human king. How can I explain to them that only you are to be king?

God: You can't, Samuel. You'll have to give them what they want. They have been asking for a king for years and years, and I'm going to let them have their way.

Samuel: But what have I done wrong? Why are they rejecting me?

God: They aren't rejecting you —they are rejecting me. They no longer want me as king. They have served other gods since I brought them out of Egypt. They are forsaking me again.

Samuel: But do they know how a king will treat them?

God: Perhaps not. Before you give them a king, be sure to warn them what a king who reigns over them will do.

(Samuel speaking to the people)

Samuel: I have spoken to God. God has agreed that you may have a king.

People: Yeah! We will have a king!

Samuel: God also commanded that I tell you what a king will do.

People: We know what a king will do! That's why we want one!

Samuel: A king will take your sons and make them into soldiers. He will force some to farm his fields and others to make weapons. Your daughters will also work for the king. He will take some of your grain and cattle and flocks.

People: We are determined to have a king over us so we will be like other nations! We want the king to govern us and go out before us to fight our battles!

Samuel: The Lord will give you your request. But it is not the Lord's choice. God wanted to be your only king.

❧ ❧ ❧

Peter Discovers God's Global Community

Based on Acts 10
(Use before session 5, part B.)

Characters:

Cornelius
Narrator
Peter

Slaves of Cornelius
The Spirit of God

Narrator: In Caesarea there was a man named Cornelius, who commanded 100 soldiers for the Romans. He was a devout man who feared God with all his household; he generously gave money and prayed constantly to God. One afternoon at about three o'clock, he had a vision in which he clearly saw an angel of God.

The Spirit: Cornelius!

Cornelius: (Terrified) What is it, Lord?

The Spirit: Your prayers and the money you have given the poor have come as an offering to God. Now send men to Joppa to find Peter, who is staying with Simon, a tanner, whose house is by the seaside.

Cornelius: He's gone! What a vision! I'll tell this to two slaves and a soldier who also serve God. Then I'll send them the 30 miles to Joppa to find this Peter.

(The next day)

Peter: I'll go up to the roof, where I can be alone, to pray while my meal is being prepared. I certainly am hungry! And it's hot up here. I'll just close my eyes to pray for a minute. *(He falls into a trance . . .)* What — what's this I see? It looks like a large sheet being low-

ered to the ground by four corners. And there are all
kinds of four-footed creatures and reptiles and birds
of the air in it. I'm hungry, and some of these would
be good to eat—the cow, the chicken, and the fish.
But some I would never eat, because our Jewish laws
have taught us that rabbits, pigs, and eagles are unclean. And they are all so mixed up I couldn't possibly
separate them!

The Spirit: Get up, Peter, kill and eat!

Peter: By no means, Lord! I have never eaten anything that
is unclean.

The Spirit: What God has made clean, you must not call unclean.

Narrator: This happened three times, and then the sheet was
suddenly taken up to heaven.

Peter: Now I realize this was a vision from God. But what
might it mean?

Slaves of Cornelius: (From the street, calling out) Is this the
house of Simon the tanner? Is Peter staying here?

The Spirit: Look, Peter, three men are searching for you. Now
get up, go down, and go with them without hesitation; for I have sent them.

Peter: *(Peering over the edge of the roof)* But they're Gentiles and one is even a soldier like those who crucified
Jesus. Why, they're unclean—oh, *(hand on forehead,
thinking hard)* so that's what the vision means! I'll go
down. *(. . . To the men)* I'm the one you're looking for.
Why have you come?

Slaves of Cornelius: Our master Cornelius, a centurion, an upright and God-fearing man, well spoken of by the
whole Jewish nation, was directed by a holy angel to
send for you to come to his house. He wants to hear
what you have to say.

Peter: I'll come, but it's too late to begin such a long journey today. Why don't you stay here with us tonight?

We'll go to Caesarea tomorrow. I'll bring some of the believers from here with me to visit Cornelius.

Narrator: The following day they came to Caesarea. Cornelius was expecting them and had called together his relatives and close friends. On Peter's arrival, Cornelius met him, and falling at his feet, worshiped him.

Peter: Stand up, Cornelius! I am only a mortal, like you. Since you've called so many together, let's go and talk to them. (*Inside, to those gathered*) You know that it is not lawful for a Jew to associate with or visit a Gentile. But God has shown me that I should not call anyone unclean. So when your messengers called on me, I came with no objection. Now may I ask why you sent for me?

Cornelius: Four days ago, at this very hour, I was praying in my house when suddenly a man in dazzling clothes stood before me. He told me to send for you, and I did. So now all of us are here in the presence of God to listen to all that the Lord has commanded you to say.

Peter: Now I truly understand that God shows no partiality, but in every nation anyone who fears him and does what is right is acceptable to him. You know the message he sent to the people of Israel, preaching peace by Jesus Christ—he is Lord of all.

Cornelius: We have heard the name of Jesus, but we don't know much about him. Pilate the governor used to live right here in Caesarea. He was never the same after he dealt with that Jesus in Jerusalem one Passover season a few years ago. If Jesus is King and Lord of all, we need to hear more. Please continue.

Peter: The message is that God anointed Jesus with the Holy Spirit and with power. Jesus went about doing good and healing, both in Judea and Jerusalem. They put him to death by hanging him on a tree; but God raised him on the third day and allowed him to appear to us who were chosen by God as witnesses.

Cornelius: So that's why the angel told me to call for you. Your witness must be blessed by heaven. We want to hear your full story.

Peter: Jesus commanded us to preach to the people and to testify that he is the one ordained by God as judge of the living and the dead. All the prophets testify about him that everyone who believes in him receives forgiveness of sins through his name.

Narrator: While Peter was still speaking, the Holy Spirit fell upon all who heard the word. The Jewish believers who had come with Peter were astounded that the gift of the Holy Spirit had been poured out even on the Gentiles, for they heard them speaking in tongues and extolling God.

Peter: Can anyone say we should not baptize with water these people who have received the Holy Spirit as we have?

Narrator: So he ordered them to be baptized in the name of Jesus Christ. Then they invited him to stay for several days.

Appendixes

1. Family Peace Education

During the buildup before the Persian Gulf War, a friend whose Christian parenting I respect came to me, a bit embarrassed. "We forgot to teach our children why we don't go to war," she confessed. "How do we start?"

I knew my friend understood peace theology—we were both students at the Associated Mennonite Biblical Seminaries in Elkhart. I recommended some stories to use as discussion starters, and she was ready for the task. But I began wondering about the many parents who couldn't easily recall the Bible passages, explain them, and add the stories of our peace heritage. How were they passing their beliefs on to their children?

The rush to educate the youth of our churches during the war was evidence that parents and churches were equally embarrassed to find that they had not taught conscientious objection to war. The purpose of this book is to improve intentional Christian peace education in the home.

Actually, I seriously doubt that my friend's children had no ideas about their parents' peace beliefs. We constantly teach our children our values whether that decision is conscious or not. Some of your conscious decisions to teach values may include:

- encouraging music lessons
- taking your children to church
- spending time in family devotions
- involving your children on ball teams
- visiting with Christian friends
- doing family service projects

These all encourage good wholesome values.

But many of our decisions are also unconscious. Our conscious decisions may collide with each other. For instance, what are we unconsciously teaching our children if our family devotion time is eliminated when friends are visiting? Or if they can't attend Bible school because of commitment to a ball team? As the too-familiar saying goes, "What we do is shouting so loudly children can't hear what we say."

Before I continue, I'll make confessions. Dennis, my husband, and I are the parents of two youngsters, Laura, seven and Joel, five. I am writing this book for parents and for children aged 10-13. I have not yet raised children this age.

Second, I have been intentional about peace education in our home. Before her third birthday, Laura was well aware that we are a "peace family." Joel has taken a bit longer, but his first response now to every religious question is "peace." Because of my work in peace education, they've picked up that this is an important part of our family's agenda.

That certainly doesn't mean we have smooth sailing! I remember poring over a magazine ad by Dakin, a company who manufactures stuffed animals. One side of the two-page spread pictured war toys, with the caption, "No wonder the jails are full." Amazed that a for-profit company would make such a bold step, I intently read the facing page, which extolled the possible nurturing values of stuffed animals. When my three-year-old son joined me, he greedily eyed the war toys, pointed to each in turn, and declared "I want that one and that one and that one. . . ."

What Is Family Peace Education?
Let's take a few minutes to discuss what family peace education is. Who does your family include? A family is increasingly hard to describe these days, but be sure to remember the influence of those living outside your home as you intentionally decide to educate your children. How can they reinforce your efforts? To help pass on your heritage, can your parents or other relatives tell stories of CPS (1940s Civilian Public Service) or I-W (1951-73 alternate service)? Are there aunts or uncles who have served overseas who can share their experiences? Possibly your family also includes those who have chosen to be involved in the military. How will you explain that decision to your children?

Where and when can this education take place? While we wish for quiet evenings gathered together around God's Word, those times may seem to exist only in an earlier era. But opportunities to discuss our response to violence are frequent if your children watch TV or go to movies, play with other children, or go to school. An article in the newspaper or a clip on a news program may give you a chance to discuss alternatives to violence. When children recount a fight on the playground or bus, you can introduce Jesus' perspective. Maybe you can recommend books which will present the issue. Your life will be the most important example, so explain to your children the decisions you make along your own faith journey.

Next we wonder just what peace is. Too often Mennonites have been known as peace-loving people only because we didn't go to war. Is that all there is to peace? The Old Testament vision was much more broad. Not only was there an absence of war, but also a presence of justice. In this vision of wholeness, everyone not only had enough to eat, but also had the opportunity to use their God-given gifts without fear.

Jesus brought the New Testament vision of peace. No longer is the dream only for a future time. *Now* is the time to love enemies, turn the other cheek, and be servants.

Peace Education Goals

How do we educate for peace? What are our goals? Stop reading and get out a piece of paper. Even a scrap will do. And a pen or pencil.

About four years ago our family had the privilege of attending a "Peace in the Family" conference at Laurelville Mennonite Center in Pennsylvania. Rich Killmer, a Presbyterian minister, encouraged us as couples to list the characteristics we hoped our children would have by age 21. Dennis and I accomplished this task some weeks after the retreat. We each made a list, compared notes, and briefly discussed them. I filed the results away and didn't look at them for two years.

Now, on your scrap of paper, do the same thing. What values do you hope your children will have by the age of 21? Because we are discussing peace education, you may want to emphasize those values, but you are welcome to add others. Peace values might include solving conflicts without violence, concern for the oppressed, a dependence on God, or belief in voluntary service as an important part of the Christian life. Jot down at least three.

Back to my story. When I discovered the list later, I was amazed to find that we had worked toward each ideal! One of our desires was that our children learn to know and trust people of other cultures and races. That fall when the newspaper printed an article about the international student-host family program at a local college, I signed us up. When Dennis and I discussed the commitment, we didn't look back at our list to decide whether it "met a goal." We knew what some of our shared family ideals were.

We also had talked about wanting to do service as a family and to use our home to serve God. Thus, when the opportunity to share our house with a Central American refugee came, we already had some ideas about our answer.

The best explanation of how we educate our children for peace is that we continue the journey ourselves and invite them along. I can talk till I'm weary about hungry children in the world, but my daughter learns best by serving beside me at a local hot meals program. When I struggle with paying our war taxes, I share my concerns and show letters I am writing to legislators. If I am unwilling to take a stand and grow myself, I am a fake to ask that of my children. And children, being who God created them to be, know it!

Moral Education
This brings us to the three E's of moral education: exhortation, example, and experience.[1] Let's imagine how we might teach that we *don't go to war.*

Exhortation is what we tell our children:
1. God created and loves everyone.
2. Jesus lived as a peacemaker.
3. Conflicts can be resolved without violence.

Example is how we as parents act:
1. Their father served as a I-W during the Vietnam War.
2. Your children know you turn to God and the Bible for answers to everyday life.
3. Your children remember your struggle about how to treat an unfair co-worker.

Experience is the opportunity we give our children:
1. We encourage them to read books with challenging ideas.
2. We provide opportunities to interact with peacemakers.
3. We invite those "different" from us to our home to give our children comfortable opportunities to learn to know them.

Intentional Education

While you may not have previously thought about intentionally teaching your children your peace beliefs, plenty of other people think the home is a primary place to begin this instruction. For instance, Deuteronomy 11:18-19 instructs parents:

> Put these words of mine in your heart and soul, and you
> shall bind them as a sign on your hand, and fix them as an
> emblem on your forehead. Teach them to your children,
> talking about them when you are at home and when you
> are away, when you lie down and when you rise.

The writer here is speaking of God's laws in general, not just the specific peace beliefs we are concentrating on. But the ideals are the same. First, the parents know the Word of God and carry it with them always. Then they are admonished to teach God's ways to their children continually, both at home and away, from the beginning of the day to the end. A tall order! God be with us!

J. C. Wenger, a Mennonite theologian, adds his feelings:

> The home is a common testing ground for the way of
> peace in everyday life. . . . In such a home, children are
> intensely aware of the central values for which their par-
> ents live, and tend to adopt those same values as they
> grow up and establish homes of their own.[2]

How can our children be "intensely aware" if instruction is only haphazard?

Finally, and perhaps surprisingly, the U.S. government also expects us to intentionally teach our peace beliefs. The third question on the Selective Service System Claim Documentation Form for conscientious objectors (COs) reads:

Describe how and when you acquired these beliefs. Your answer may include such information as the influence of family members or other persons; training, if applicable; your personal experiences; membership in organizations; books and readings which influenced you.

By the age of 18, the government expects our young people to be able to trace the development of their conscientious objection to war. For ideas on how to create a CO file with your child, see appendix 4 under "Draft Counseling." Congratulations! By picking up this book, you've intentionally decided to begin that process!

Foundations for Peace Education

Now that we've examined some of the hows and whys, let's look at the basis of our peace education. Our belief in not going to war, and thus this book's premise, is that God, as shown through the Bible and the life, death, and resurrection of Jesus, is the God of peace. As you work through the sessions, you will find numerous Bible verses cited. The evidence in both the Old and New Testaments is heavy: God's best way is the way of peace.

Our understanding of theology also draws on the continuing story of God's people. As Mennonites, for example, we trace our ancestry to the Anabaptists. Their story is our heritage and a foundation of the education we give our children. Other denominations have their own traditions.

But the story of God's people hasn't ended, so our comprehension of peace theology is continually enriched. As circumstances around our people have changed, so has some of our perception of how God works in the world. Be assured—I do not believe God changes! But I do believe that our puny minds cannot fully understand the magnitude of God's ways. Thus, there is always a bit more of God's character left for us to discover. For new insights we turn to our contemporaries who

> **But to pray for peace, Christians
> believe, is more than just to meditate
> on the meaning of peace. . . . It is to
> bring into the human situation the very
> power of the God of peace, or, better
> expressed, to open up our human
> situation to that power.**
> —*John Macquarrie*[3]

struggle to understand God's answer to modern violence and injustice.

Always, as we educate our children and live our own complicated lives, we depend on God. Prayer is the evidence of this dependence. Prayer brings us to the safety of God's presence and is thus the first step both in our understanding of peace and our choice to pass the belief on to our children.

There are then four basic foundations for peace theology: (1) God's love as revealed through the Bible and Jesus, (2) our church history, (3) the struggles of contemporary peacemakers, and (4) our own relationship with God.

Principles of Family Peace Education

Wonderful books have been written on family peace education, and I'll only whet your appetite here. The book I especially appreciate is *Parenting for Peace and Justice: Ten Years Later*, by Kathleen and James McGinnis; and the booklet *How to Teach Peace to Children*, by J. Lorne Peachey (see appendix 2). My thinking has been so guided by these authors that their ideas are inseparably intertwined with mine. The first time I checked the McGinnis book out of our church library, we didn't even have children. I kept the book so long the librarian finally tracked me down. I confessed that I'd been reading it over and over, hoping the insights would become firmly embedded in my mind, so that when we did have children, these ideals would come naturally.

Affirmation
Some describe our society as drunk with violence. Raising our children to have Christian peace values is to raise them to be different from their peers. The most important gift we can give our children on this difficult journey is affirmation.

For entirely too long, Mennonites have confused affirming their children with instilling them with pride. We need to remember that the very basis of feeling good about ourselves comes from our relationship with Jesus. God loves us no matter what, and finds us to be so worthwhile that he sent his Son to die for our sins. We don't earn this gift (that would be pride); we are given it freely. For these same reasons, we love and affirm our children, teaching them that they are worthwhile and lovable. This is true affirmation.

To have the courage to go against their culture, children need a secure homelife and good self-esteem. The basis for this security is the parents' relationship and the tone they set for the home. A friend recently described her family as "fun to belong to." Children need to feel good about the group they are a part of. They need to know they *belong.*

How do you cultivate a special feeling about your family? First, you can emphasize family traditions. When our children were young, neighbors were visiting on April 1. I prepared brownies containing rubber bands for lunch. At the beginning of the meal, I placed the brownies on upside-down plates and declared, "You may *not* have the rest of your meal until you have cleaned up your plates." Mass hilarity resulted.

I thought that was the end of the idea, but my daughter remembered the "tradition" the following year. April 1 fell on a Sunday, and as luck shines on our family, an all-church carry-in was planned for that day. Laura insisted that we make a chocolate cake, complete with rubber bands, as our contribution, and for some odd reason, I consented. During their first trip through the potluck line, the children proceeded to choose only deserts and were soon happily picking their way around the cake with rubber bands. After a wide-eyed friend observed what they were doing, she pointed out what I had not realized: Some of the older members of our congregation would not easily see the rubber bands (and I had chosen enormous ones on purpose!) nor discover them in their mouths because of dentures. With a face as red as the punch being served, I trudged up and down the tables pointing out the special cake to everyone and imploring them to be careful. What a family to belong to!

While your traditions may be less crazy, be sure they emphasize the specialness of family and the joy of belonging to each other.

Another gift of affirmation to our children is letting them know they are capable. The best way to pass on this tidbit is by giving children tasks (chores) so they feel both a sense of accomplishment and the ability to contribute to family life. Jobs around the house can meet two goals. We can set our children up to succeed by giving them assignments they can do well. But we can also help stretch their abilities up a notch by giving them tasks that make them strive. Both purposes will be defeated if children are frustrated, and so we have to be sure our requests are age appropriate.

My grandfather discovered this the hard way. He had a stroke soon after I was born and found walking difficult the rest of his years. When I was two, he asked me to bring him a drink of water. I resourcefully got a doll teacup and made several trips to quench his thirst. When my father came upon the scene, he remarked, "Dad, think a minute. Where is the only place in the house she can reach to get water?" My grandfather turned several shades of green and learned a bit about age-appropriate tasks.

I've tried to teach the children that there are various kinds of work to do. Daddy is a schoolteacher, and his job is to teach English and run the library. Mommy is a peace and justice educator, and her job is to help others learn the way of peace. The children are students, and their work is to learn at school. But there are many jobs to be done at home that are family tasks: cooking, setting the table, cleaning, doing laundry, yard work. They don't belong exclusively to the parents. I don't ask my children to "help me" unless it is a job that really belongs to me. Rather, I ask them to do their share of the family work so that we can all get finished together. I'll have to wait until the children are older to discover if this semantic twist helps!

Third, children need to know they are loved and cherished. They have to be assured that when they make mistakes, they will still be accepted. Making peace is creative and dangerous! Children gain courage from knowing that even if they fail, they will be loved and encouraged to continue trying.

Helping children understand their emotions also affirms them for who they are. Our willingness to respect our children's feelings enables them to trust that part of themselves and to feel comfortable with others' feelings. Encourage your children to find acceptable ways of dealing with difficult emotions. Denying emotions ("no, you don't really mean that") doesn't make them go away.

Nonviolence in the Home
If we expect our children to be nonviolent, our homelife must lay the groundwork. It can begin with the use of authority in the home. If children feel respected and understood by their parents, they will learn to use authority justly. Polly Berrien Berends puts it succinctly, "The important thing is for children and parents to become aware of God as the parent rather than feeling that parents are God."[4]

How we resolve conflicts in the home is great training ground for the world. At a workshop with students in grades 4-8, one boy talked about a continual conflict with his mother over tracking mud through the house. His mother was becoming increasingly angry about the time it took her to clean up the mud. She was present as a sponsor, so together we all brainstormed possible "win-win" solutions.

The first idea was that he not wear his shoes in the house, but the mother was quick to point out that if he could learn to do this, there wouldn't be the long-standing problem. The second idea was that he learn to clean up after himself. This would then give his mother extra time and a better disposition. Did he have any ideas as to how he'd like her to spend that bonus time?

He pounced. "I want her to play more Ping-Pong with me." We set up a reward system: for so many clean-floor days with no reminders, she would play Ping-Pong for so long. I suggested that they may want to reevaluate the plan eventually so that it would continue to meet their needs. "You don't want this to last even after you leave home," I explained. "Why not?" the son countered. "I'll still want to play Ping-Pong with her when I come home to visit!"

We are role models for our children, and they are continually observing how we handle conflict in the home, react to it in the community, and relate to our violent world. A quick course in conflict resolution skills includes the following:

1. Listening effectively by feeding back what you heard: "Are you saying you are angry because I asked you to pick up your clothes?"

2. Expressing how you feel rather than pointing the finger at others: "I get angry when I'm not listened to," rather than "You lazy oaf!"

3. Working together to see how the conflict can be resolved so that everyone involved is satisfied.

4. Deciding how to check up later on the conflict to be sure it has been resolved.

Doug Penner explains, "In the midst of . . . interpersonal strains, it may be helpful to be aware of a few general principles related to conflict and peacemaking . . . : (1) that our commitments to peace and justice are as relevant to personal relationships as they are to relationships between nations, and (2) that positive things can happen when people are able to engage in honest, direct discussion of issues they disagree about and still maintain a relationship.[5]

Many families find that regular family meetings keep communication open. We have found this to happen most naturally around the dinner table. We've only practiced the meetings sporadically, but even our young children were excited about the opportunity to voice their opinions with the entire family's full attention. The McGinnis writings have many suggestions to make this a successful venture.

Encourage cooperation between family members and friends rather than competition, which often leads to winners, losers, and upset feelings. Neither of our children enjoyed taking the garbage down to the compost pile and continually argued about whose turn it was. I finally assigned one of them the task of carrying the bucket down and the other that of bringing it back up. Now, instead of tears of protest, I hear the children's laughter as they come back from the garden hand-in-hand. Well, at least sometimes!

Along the same lines, emphasize the joy of playing rather than the outcome. "Did you have fun playing soccer?" rather than the almost inevitable, "Who won?" Encourage situations where children almost naturally cooperate, like building sand castles or preparing a group hero sandwich. Avoid comparing one child's efforts to another's.

Don't Glorify War
How obvious this principle seems! If we are teaching peace, we won't paint a rosy picture of war. But wait—our children all too often see us dabbling in the "forbidden."

When I taught in a Mennonite high school, an earnest and dynamic young man who had decided not to register for the 1980 draft registration came to speak in chapel. His enthusiasm was contagious and his reasoning strong. A local minister asked for equal time to explain submission to the government. He began his chapel talk by explaining his fascination with bombers during World War II and how he had carefully memorized the capabilities of each one. He lost his credibility long before getting to the meat of his message. After hearing from a young man willing to risk his future career to follow his conscience, the students had little patience with a man whose interests followed violence.

Common ways parents glorify war in the home include the movies and TV they watch. Children even as old as late elementary age can't separate the evil of killing in real life from the enjoyment of watching clean killing on TV. These depictions imply that death can be quick and simple.

My husband, Dennis, teaches high school English, and the junior class studies *All Quiet on the Western Front* via videotape. One scene includes a soldier trapped in a foxhole with a man he rammed with a bayonet. The man dies incredibly slowly, and several minutes of screen time are devoted to his agony. Dennis reports that few students can concentrate on the screen the entire time. While these youth have reportedly seen hundreds of deaths on TV by this age, none have acquainted them with realistic, painful death. They didn't know it could be so horrible.

Inevitably, this discussion leads us to consider war toys. I do not understand why it might be okay to pretend to do something in the backyard against which I'm teaching in real life. *Who's Calling the Shots*, by Nancy Carlsson-Paige and Diane E. Levin,[6] points out how war play and war toys have changed since we were children. Today many of these toys complement cartoon scripts (written by adults) which the children have memorized. Instead of acting out their own hostilities and enriching their ability to pretend, children are simply reenacting a program they've seen. This is a totally different game. Many public schools and preschools have outlawed these toys because they seem to encourage violence among children. Can not we as Christian peacemakers take a similar stand?

At our house, deciding not to have war toys has not been easy, and since Joel is only five, the unrest is not over. The truce has included the following:

1. I will not buy or provide toys for my children I do not approve of.

2. Our property is a "No war-toys zone." If others bring these toys to our home, they sit in a corner until the child leaves.

3. When we read through the Laura Ingalls Wilder books, the children discovered that guns are sometimes used to protect us from wild animals. I've encouraged Joel to use the guns he fashions himself against animals. One may never point a gun at a human being, created by God!

4. When Joel creates a war toy, I suggest alternate uses. "Yes, that plane can be used for dropping bombs, but let's think of something dangerous, yet helpful, it could be doing. How about trying to put out forest fires?" This emphasis and our recent talks about hunger in Somalia led him to "play" filling trucks with rice for MCC (Mennonite Central Committee) to take to hungry people. Children can only play what they've been exposed to!

5. I try not to dictate what toys Joel plays with at other people's houses. He must deal with his own conscience when he is away from me.

6. Recently I was in Haiti with a Christian Peacemaker Team. Just before I left, Joel expressed concern that I might get shot. I promised that I would not willingly go where this was a possibility. The pledge was not easy to keep. Now when Joel wants to shoot at others, I point out that it isn't fair for him to use a gun after his request. Reality has been the best teacher.

A final way we glorify violence and confuse our children is by the heroes we choose. Do we offer alternatives to the studies at school of "greats" who led armies to battle and conquered native peoples?

Emphasize Peace

After reviewing the slippery ways we might glorify violence, let's revel in ways to relish peace. We can encourage our children to form friendships with other peacemakers. When these folks come through, we can open our homes to host them and invite others to meet them. Laura has been a fan of *Road Less Travelled* and their children's "I Can Make Peace" tape for years (see appendix 2). When they performed at our church, she decided to pack a small bag of goodies for them to take to their next stop. Somehow Jude Krehbiel found our address and wrote her a thank-you note for this simple gift. This certainly brought Laura a step further on her journey of peace.

> It is not enough to say, 'We must not wage war!' It is necessary to love peace and sacrifice for it. We must concentrate not on the eradication of war but on the affirmation of peace.
> —*Martin Luther King*[7]

If you have trouble meeting peacemakers in person, turn to their stories and books. This book includes stories as part of each session and suggestions for further reading. Help your children find peace heroes for inspiration. The best of those is Jesus.

Support peace projects with your family finances and time. MCC has a Global Family Project which will pair you with children who need help to complete their education. They also can direct your money toward those who are aching because of war and violence.[8]

A last way is to own peace materials. One night in Oregon I was privileged to stay in the home of some folks who had served in Kampuchea. Just walking into their home informed me that they had worked with MCC. Calendars had pictures of children around the world and peace quotations. Shelves overflowed with simple cooking and living books. Banners and crafts came from many nations. Posters proclaimed the way of peace. Their home was an open invitation to move beyond our small communities and seek God's justice in the world.

Enjoy God's Global Community

I find this to be such a central part of the gospel of peace that I've devoted an entire session to it. I believe that Jesus died and was raised to restore my relationship not only with God, but also with those around the world who I perceive to be different from me. God created and made all peoples, so we are more similar than different. Our diversity reflects the infinity of God's imagination. People around the world worship God according to their culture, showing us different faces of God's character.

One of my most poignant experiences of learning how God answers people's many different needs occurred while I was in Honduras on Study-Service Trimester with Goshen College. I had endured many masses while there and hadn't understood a single one because my Spanish was limited and my understanding of the Catholic faith even more restricted. Finally I had the opportunity to attend a mass in English in celebration of a Sister's 55th anniversary of taking her vows. Although the Sister had been working in Honduras for nearly a year, she spoke almost no Spanish.

I came to that mass with high expectations of learning to know the God these good Sisters worshiped. I was quite chagrined to discover that the priest had decided to say the mass in Spanish because some Honduran sisters had traveled quite a distance to be there and he didn't want to disappoint them. However, in the midst of that devout gathering, when the priest rang the bell, I understood in a flash that God was meeting the needs of these believers. I have no careful theological explanation for what happened to that bread, but I understood God to clearly say to me that he was nourishing these Sisters' souls. And my understanding of God leaped forward.

Live Responsibly

The more-with-less movement has been making its mark widely,[9] but many Christians seem to have joined mainstream materialism. Part of your journey to justice should include reviewing the responsible living (no one with a family has ever called it simple!) books you or your church library has stashed away. While we tire of hearing the statistics repeated, we need to be reminded that Americans use too many resources. Too often, these many possessions create in us a need to protect what we own. This can lead to war. Protecting a way of life and our access to oil were some of the reasons for the Persian Gulf War.

Live simply that others may simply live.[10]

Care for God's Earth

Many Christians have been tireless workers in the ecology movement and with good reason—we serve the Master Creator. These folks have discovered that we are the caretakers of the earth, not the masters. Involve your children in your work. When I pushed strollers with the children around the block, we took a sack along to place litter in. We didn't find all that much, but the children did learn that our job was to pick up after others, not create a mess. We'd sing "Here we go a walkin', walkin', walkin'. Here we go a walkin', cleaning up God's world." I wanted the connection to be firmly ingrained in their minds.

Now we live outside town and the children have outgrown strollers. But Laura looked out the window one day and saw a smokestack giving off steam. "Let's tell those people to stop polluting!" she declared. "Tell them yourself," I replied. "That's our electric plant, and the less electricity we waste, the less coal they'll burn to pollute the air." For several days, I had an energetic helper turning lights off—whether we were finished or not!

Publicly Work for Justice

I believe families without a mission beyond themselves tend to become in-grown and self-centered. Here is how Richard Killmer explains it:[11]

> The family is not just a little redeemed community which sits isolated from the world. The family is also a means of redemption —a means by which God is at work in the world granting peace. The family not only seeks its own solidarity (which it certainly needs to build) but it reaches out to the whole world pointing to and becoming a part of God's peacegiving. . . . In fact peace in the family is not possible if we ignore the task of peacemaking in the world beyond our family.

Killmer then went on to quote David Willis. The tight wording of this makes it one of my all-time favorites.

> Without some sense of calling as a family to a higher cause beyond itself, a family easily becomes sticky and suffocating. Mother love becomes smother worry, father love becomes patriarchal authoritarianism, childhood becomes consumer tyranny, brotherhood and sisterhood become boot-camp training for the battle of the sexes.

Just as a church with no mission is dead, so a family which only looks inward begins to feed upon itself. When all my attention is focused on how things are going at home, I magnify the problems. But when our family together is working to ease someone else's misery, our own problems seem just a bit smaller. I will admit that I have trouble finding the fine balance between looking inward and looking outward and have at times overextended our resources.

> It may well be that the greatest tragedy of this period of social transition is not the glaring noisiness of the so-called bad people, but the appalling silence of the so-called good people.
>
> —*Martin Luther King, Jr.*[12]

The Path to Peace

Let me repeat that we seek a consistent environment, one which extols the virtues of peace in all we say and do. I too often fall short of my own goals and ideals, and I have waking nightmares of my children joining me at a workshop and revealing my shortcomings. "That's what she says, but you should see what she actually *does!*" When, inevitably, I make mistakes, I try to explain those to the children as well, so they realize this is not the way I truly want to live.

I must talk a bit about celebrations. I think my parents' generation and perhaps some of mine grew up with a peace position based on a series of no's. "No, you can't march in the July 4 parade; that glorifies a war." "No, you can't become a girl scout. Their main purpose is to train good U.S. citizens." "No, you can't watch that program—it's too violent." "No, you can't buy that toy because it is used to kill."

Now, more or less, I agree with the sentiment of these statements (such an old fogy I am!), but disagree with the tone of voice. You see, we must never forget that we are not *just* saying no! to war. Much more importantly, we are saying YES!!! to life, and not just any life, but the fullness of life Jesus offers us. I would rephrase the no's this way:

"This year our family will be celebrating the interdependence of the world on July 4. Which of your friends would you like to invite for the party?" "Our church is beginning a special mentoring program. Whom would you like to be your mentor?" "Come, join me in the kitchen, and we can make your favorite cookies. We'll make enough so we can share some with whomever you'd like." "Let's buy this game we can all play together. Remember, since it's a cooperative game, we either all win or all lose." And make time to celebrate!

We are all on a journey, taking steps along the path of peace. It really doesn't matter where we are on that path, only that we are preparing for the next step. The danger is staying in the same place too long. God bless you and the children you are nurturing as you walk along together.

No one has a right to sit down and feel hopeless. There's too much work to do.

—Dorothy Day[13]

2. Family Peace Education Resources

(Also see resources in appendix 5.)

Book Companies
Alternatives, Box 429, Ellenwood, GA 30049 (404 961-0102).
    Celebration specialists!
Provident Bookstores, Lancaster Shopping Center, 1625 Lititz
    Pike, Lancaster, PA 17601-6599 (800 759-4447; 717 397-
    3517).

Conflict Resolution
Fighting Fair for Families, by Fran Schmidt and Alice Fried-
    man. Grace Contrino Abrams Peace Education Founda-
    tion, Inc., PO Box 191153, Miami Beach, FL 33119, 1989.

Cooperative Games
Animal Town, PO Box 485, Healdsburg, CA 95448-0485 (800
    445-8642).
Family Pastimes, RR 4, Perth, ON K7H 3C6, Canada (613 267-
    4819).

International Resources
Crafts: MCC, 21 S. 12th Street, PO Box 500, Akron, PA 17501-
    0500.
Food: *Extending the Table*, by Joetta Handrich Schlabach.
    Scottdale, Pa.: Herald Press, 1991.
Pen Pals: Kids Meeting Kids, Box 8H, 380 Riverside Drive,
    New York, NY 10025.

Music
"Road Less Travelled," peace and justice concerts and
    cassettes for all ages, by Doug and Jude Krehbiel. 67660
    Valley Road, White Pigeon, MI 49099 (616 641-7873).
Teaching Peace, by Red Grammer. Smilin' Atcha, 939 Orchard
    St., Peekskill, NY 10566.

Parenting

*Growing Toward Peace: Stories from Teachers and Parents
About Real Children Learning to Live Peacefully*, ed. by
Kathryn Aschliman. Scottdale, Pa.: Herald Press, 1993.
How to Teach Peace to Children, by J. Lorne Peachey.
Scottdale, Pa.: Herald Press, 1981.
Parenting for Peace and Justice: Ten Years Later, by James and
Kathleen McGinnis. Rev. ed. Maryknoll, N.Y.: Orbis, 1989.

Peace Stories

Coals of Fire, by Elizabeth Hershberger Bauman. Scottdale,
Pa.: Herald Press, 1954, 1982.
Dial 911: Peaceful Christians and Urban Violence, by Dave
Jackson. Scottdale, Pa.: Herald Press, 1981.
The Friendly Caravan, by a committee. Wallingford, Pa.:
Pendle Hill Publications, 1990.
I Heard Good News Today, by Cornelia Lehn. Newton, Kan.:
Faith & Life Press, 1983.
Peace Be with You, by Cornelia Lehn. Newton, Kan.: Faith &
Life Press, 1980.
Seeking Peace, by Titus and Linda Peachey. Intercourse, Pa.:
Good Books, 1991.
They Loved Their Enemies, by Marian Hostetler. Scottdale,
Pa.: Herald Press, 1988.
Walking with Jesus, by Mary Clemens Meyer. Scottdale, Pa.:
Herald Press, 1992.

Posters

Church World Service (CWS), PO Box 968, 28606 Phillips St.,
Elkhart, IN 46515.
Fellowship of Reconciliation (FOR), Box 271, Nyack, NY
10960.
Mennonite Central Committee (MCC), 21 S. 12th Street, PO
Box 500, Akron, PA 17501-0500.

Stop War Toys Campaign

New England War Resistors League, Box 1093, Norwich, CT
06360 (508 774-3417). Send for a packet of ideas about
war toys.

Touchable Globes

Commission on Overseas Mission, 722 Main Street, Box 347,
Newton, KS 67114-0347 (316 283-5100). A 27" beach ball
globe with countries and cities, for $13 plus postage;
smaller sizes also available.

16" Whole Earth ball: Third World Shoppe, 611 West Wayne,
Fort Wayne, IN 46802; as photographed by astronauts;
$8.95 plus postage.

Hugg-a-Planet: XTC Products Inc, 247 Rockingstone Ave.,
Larchmont, NY 19538 (914 833-0200).

3. Family Peace Projects

1. Birthdays

Children love birthdays. Celebrating the birth dates of peace-makers is one way to capture your children's imagination and enthusiasm. We've done this twice. The first time, when the children were quite small, we celebrated Harriet Tubman's birthday. I realized that all our children's dolls were white and went to a post-Christmas sale of toys. Then we read a library book about Tubman and had a cake. I gave each of the children a black doll in honor of Tubman. Joel was too young to talk. Laura promptly named hers "Harriet" and Joel's "Moses." (Curiously, I had never explained to the children that Harriet Tubman was called the Moses of her people.)

That party was a much bigger hit than the one last fall for Mother Teresa. Hoping to impress upon the children Mother Teresa's love for the poor, I emphasized food typical and cheap in India. The simple lentils and rice had quite the opposite effect on my children aged four and six, and they quickly decided they would *never* follow her footsteps!

Here are a few dates to get you started, but don't limit the fun!

January 15	Martin Luther King's birthday
January 30	Mahatma Gandhi assassinated, 1948
March 10	Harriet Tubman Day
March 12	21-year-old Maximilianus executed
March 24	Oscar Romero assassinated
May 9	Daniel Berrigan, born 1921
August 27	Mother Teresa, born 1910
September 6	Jane Addams, born 1860
September 22	Raoul Wallenberg Day
October 4	St. Francis of Assisi Day
November 8	Dorothy Day, born 1897
November 11	Martin of Tours Day
November 14	Booker T. Washington (birth and death day)

2. Videos

Mennonite Central Committee has free videos available. Many include discussion guides. All you pay is the return postage. Their catalog is also free. Here are a few suggestions, paired with sessions numbered in parentheses:

Peace Awareness for Children
(1) *How Do You Spell Peace?* (slide set)
(4) *I Hope They Don't Bomb my Lilypad* (filmstrip)
Conflict Resolution
Fighting Fair: Dr. Martin Luther King, Jr., for Kids
Nuclear War
Buster and Me
Butter Battle Book
(5) Prejudice
The Unforgettable Pen Pal
It's So Nice to Have a Wolf Around the House (film)
(5) Children Around the World
Children's Fun in Lesotho (slide set)
The World's Children (films/videos of children in Nepal, Bolivia, Kenya, Thailand, Peru, St. Vincent, and Philippines)
Refugees: Friends Without a Home (filmstrips)
(5-6) Children Who Make Peace
Sadako Sasaki and the Paper Cranes (slide set)
I Can Make a Difference (slide set)
Children Creating Peace
(6) Hunger
Hunger in Our World Family: We Can Help! (slide set)
Sights and Sounds of Hunger (filmstrips)
(6) How MCC Helps
No Kidding Cartoons
Water: The Life-giving Resource (filmstrips)

3. Interdependence Day (5)

One year we celebrated "Interdependence Day" on July 4. Our goal was to point out how much we have gained from our relationship to the world community. We invited friends with overseas experience to bring foods with a foreign flavor for lunch. Afterward we gathered around our huge globe and told stories of our times overseas. Try to help friends concentrate on what insights they gained from the other culture, perhaps about God or relationships.

4. King Jesus Party (3)

How can we celebrate our trust in God? With a King Jesus Party! Your family can reenact the Palm Sunday parade and then serve a special meal, recognizing that Jesus is among you. Set a special place, and let the children decorate for the honored guest. Sing songs of praise. Use the evening to heighten awareness that Jesus is always with us.

5. Letter Writing (3)

One way to help your children review their learnings is by inviting them to write a letter to their legislators at the same time you do. They can explain why they don't want their country to go to war or use tax money for armaments. Encourage them to state specific reasons. They can anticipate a reply several weeks (sometimes months) after mailing the letter.

6. Cross-Cultural Experiences (5)

Provide your children with comfortable experiences with people from races or cultures other than your own. Doing this in the safety of your home gives children security as they deal with differences. Also take part in local cultural events which broaden your children's understanding.

7. Christmas and Easter (3)

Analyze your Christmas and Easter celebrations. Is the kingship of Jesus evident, or must one wade through the gods of materialism and abundance to find him? Can your children sort out what you are celebrating? Alternatives (see appendix 2) has many excellent resources.

8. Service Projects (6)
Possibilities abound for service projects and vacations with a purpose. Contact your pastor, local ministerial association, or your conference office for ideas. Build an expectation that your family members regularly perform service together.

9. Banners (1-6)
Create banners to accompany each session. Use the memory verses or other phrases that sum up what the youth have learned. Choose a central location to hang one and change it frequently. If your family tires of them, give them to others.

10. Peacebook (1-6)
Start your own "Peacebook"! Make or buy a special blank book, and record important peacemaking events from your family life. This will recognize your children's growing understandings. If they later need to defend their peace position before a draft board, this will serve as an excellent witness.

11. Peace Cards (1-6)
Celebrate holidays and birthdays by sending handmade cards with peace themes to family and friends.

12. News Analysis (1-6)
Listen to the news with your children and analyze together the injustices of the world and what God's will might be.

13. Shelter Someone (6)
Invite someone needing nurture and shelter to live with your family. This might be a pregnant teen, an MCC volunteer, an older person no longer able to live alone, or a refugee.

14. Song (1-6)
Create your own family song about peace. First choose the major ideas you want to express, decide on a suitable chorus, then explode with rhythm and tune!

15. Contributions (1-6)
Invite your children to help decide family charitable contributions. Choose from MCC projects (see MCC's "Sharing Calendar" and giving cube), your local crisis pregnancy center, grocery distribution, hot meal program, education for minority youth, and other favorite causes. Consider sending an annual gift to NISBCO (National Interreligious Service Board for Conscientious Objectors), or MCC (Mennonite Central Committee), or the Peace Tax Fund (for addresses, see appendix 5).

In your "Peacebook," record that you "put your money where your heart is" as further evidence of your sincere CO (conscientious objector) beliefs. Some families save all appeals they receive and quarterly make decisions together. Help your children understand how responsibly organizations use their money and what part is used for publicity or high salaries.

16. Christian Peacemaker Teams (1, 2, 6)
Support Christian Peacemaker Teams (CPT: 1821 W. Cullerton, Chicago, IL 60608; 312 421-5513), an organization associated with the Church of the Brethren and Mennonite churches, which works for Peace and Justice. Discover when they will next send a group on a mission overseas, and invite your children to write letters and draw pictures CPT can give as gifts to those they meet. Pray for their work, and add them to your family's contribution list.

17. Museums and Restaurants (5)
Visit local art museums or ethnic museums and restaurants for exposure to other cultures. Collect Christian art work from around the world for different views of God.

18. Demonstrations (6)

Take the children along if you take part in a safe demonstration for peace. Be sure the placards you carry clearly explain your reasons for involvement as a Christian.

19. Video Making (1-6)

Make a family peace video. Act out one of the stories or Bible passages used in the book, another favorite story you've discovered, or create your own. Or give a live dramatization at a family reunion or church gathering.

20. Peace Holidays (1-6)

Other "Peace Holidays" abound:

January	Black History Month
January 1	World Day of Prayer for Peace
January 21-22	National Prayer Vigil for Life
March 8	International Women's Day
April 22	Earth Day
September 15	Begins Hispanic Heritage Week
September 28	Native American Day
October 16-24	Peace with Justice Week
October 16	World Food Day
December 9	National Human Rights Day

4. Congregational Peace Education

Let's go back to Paul's image of the plant from Corinthians that we used at the end of the introduction to the book. There we emphasized that while parents plant the seeds of peace in their youth and the congregation waters them, only God gives the growth. The question now is, How does the congregation best do the watering?

Peace Education

What is congregational peace education? It is biblically based and Holy Spirit-driven teaching which increases understanding and the amount of peace and justice in the world. What a mouthful! Like all other education in a congregation, we teach peace and justice because of our understanding of who God is, the message Jesus brought when he lived, died, and was raised, and the nudgings (and outright shoves!) of the Holy Spirit.

Peace education is not something we hurry to give our youth just before they turn eighteen and must face registration or a draft. During the Persian Gulf War, some adults went so far as to admit, "We need a good war every generation to keep the peace position strong."

If peace education happens only in such an emergency situation, we've lost the point. Peace is a total lifestyle, a radically new approach to living. Perhaps one of its most obvious characteristics is refusing to serve in the armed forces, but others include how we make, spend, and invest money; our relationships with others, our use of time, and how we worship. Thus, peace education will address all these, reach all ages, and be a part of the congregation's teaching cycle. If youth don't see adults continuing to struggle and grow in their understanding of peace and justice as they live in society, they will resent learnings which set them apart from their peers.

The Congregation

Who is this congregation we've laid such a heavy job on? Likely it is the group with whom you worship on Sunday mornings. To do effective peace education, this gathering will do three things for you and your children: affirm the use of your gifts, support your nonconformity to the world, and encourage you to take the next step on the path of peace. While the job sounds impossibly big, the joy is that God leads and the congregation need only be open to following.

The wheres and whens of congregational peace education are somewhat obvious. We expect it to take place in the congregation's meetinghouse, the homes of other members, at church outings and summer camps. The Sunday morning worship service and Sunday school, Sunday or Wednesday evening services, and Bible school—all these occasions can provide instruction on a regular basis.

One year my home congregation, Oak Grove Mennonite, Smithville, Ohio, emphasized peace during our Bible school. Our openings included puppet shows from the *Friendly Creature Features*, a conflict resolution series; an MCC (Mennonite Central Committee) offering project for Central American children living in refugee camps as a result of war; cooperative games on the playground (the recreation director noticed a definite decrease in fights and bickering); special peace classes for each age-group; and peace buttons. The teachers began each day wearing the buttons, and as soon as they saw a student making peace, they gave a button to that person, who then passed it on to another peacemaker caught in the act. At the end of the day, they reviewed these acts: the last person wearing the button explained the peace action recognized, then passed the peace button back up the chain of peacemakers, who each told their story.

Don't get me wrong! A congregation which has a peace Bible school every year is missing out on giving other necessary Christian education. But the congregation which never makes it a special emphasis is also being negligent.

In a similar vein, a preacher who tackles the peace lifestyle and its biblical basis in sermon after sermon is not providing a balanced understanding of the Bible. But at least once a year, perhaps on Peace Sunday (for Mennonites, the Sunday closest to July 4), or during Peace and Justice Week (October 16-24), a stirring sermon is appropriate.

Special Traditions

Special traditions mark a congregation as interested in teaching peace. The most popular at Oak Grove is our Peace Campfire, perhaps a loose connection to the book, *Coals of Fire* (see Bibliography). On a fall Sunday afternoon, all ages gather for intergenerational games. The year we borrowed a parachute was the biggest success. We then enjoy a carry-in meal with roasted hot dogs followed by a program around the campfire. This is a time for telling peace stories and singing, with something included for all ages. One year we dedicated a Peace Pole; another year we shared poems, pictures, skits, and other crafts on the theme. This is followed by popcorn over the fire.

Another special intergenerational event is Peace Reading Month. All the peace books from the library and some from private collections[1] are placed on a table. All ages are encouraged to read at least a book during the month. At the culminating Sunday evening service, "book reports" are given. Some children prefer to draw a picture and have their parents explain it. Everyone who reads a book gets a prize, and refreshments are served. One year gummy "bookworms" were a big hit. Unexpected benefits are a chance for the children to speak publicly and for the older adults to become better acquainted with them.

Other ideas for congregational peace education abound. See the list at the end of this section for books to use. The important point is that we must be deliberate and intentional. It must be a planned part of the congregation's life, not an "Oh, oh!" when a war comes along or a youth decides to volunteer for the military.

Congregations must also be consistent with their messages. If they insist that countries should not solve conflict with war, neither should they solve problems by splitting and harboring angry feelings. Church is the perfect place to teach concrete conflict resolution skills.

What then do we want this congregational peace education to accomplish? We've already touched on one point: an understanding of the biblical foundation. We also hope our congregations pass on a knowledge of church history, affirmation for Christian peacemaking, and a reinforcement of God's love to all peoples. The concept of stewardship should be examined and service emphasized.

Draft Counseling

Congregations who encourage youth to take the CO stand should designate a draft counselor. This person needs both to stay up-to-date with current legislation and to know the youth of the congregation and their feelings and understandings. In their budgets, congregations should also include the groups (CCCO, MCC, NISBCO; for addresses see appendix 5) which follow draft legislation and make this information available. This keeps the groups visible and gives them a much-needed base of support.

No later than when teens, both male and female, turn 16, draft counselors should explain the registration and draft laws of the country. Teens will already understand the biblical basis and lifestyle choices of the conscientious objector because their congregations have prepared them. They are now ready to tackle the system.

First, they should begin a CO file to record the evolution of their beliefs and demonstrate their sincerity. This file can include records of their actions for peace and justice, including involvement in groups organized for peace; reports on books which influenced their CO thinking; school papers; explanations of how the beliefs of others have influenced them; and letters of support from members of the congregation, especially including the pastor.

The next steps are to fill out the Peacemaker Registration Form, available from MCC, and prepare for a Draft Board Hearing. Before the time comes for eighteen-year-olds actually to register, they should complete the draft counseling procedure. Contact NISBCO or MCC for more information.

Peace congregations should not only protect their own teens from serving in the military. They should also understand local recruiting practices and the desperation which leads some youth to volunteer. Contact CCCO, MCC, or NISBCO to see how your congregation can be involved in counter-recruitment or supporting those who decide they are COs after they join the military. These are important opportunities for witness and service.

The Path to Peace
An MCC pamphlet "Christians and War" ends this way:

> Many times, Christians who look for alternatives to war hope to find easy alternatives. But there are no easy paths to peace. The way of peace is marked by the suffering of people who chose not to take up weapons against an "enemy." Although many peace-promoting activities are pleasant, happy experiences, a commitment to a life of peace will be demanding, time consuming, and costly.

The job of our congregations is to prepare us all for this path of peace and support us on the way.

5. Congregational Peace Education Resources

(Also see resources in appendix 2.)

Curriculum for Sunday/Bible School, Sunday Evening Grades 1-8 (and up)

Becoming God's Peacemakers, by Suella L. Gerber, Kathleen K. Janssen, and Rosemary G. Widmer. Newton, Kan.: Faith & Life Press, 1992.

Educating for Peace and Justice: Religious Dimensions, by James McGinnis. Vol. 1, grades K-6; vol. 2, grades 7-12. St. Louis, Mo.: Institute for Peace and Justice, 1993.

Friendly Creature Features: Puppet Shows and Conflict Resolution workshops for Primary Grade Children, by Mary Finn and Rosemary Murray. Western New York Peace Center, 472 Emslie, Buffalo, NY 14212, 1985.

Helping Families Care: Practical Ideas for Integenerational Programs, by James McGinnis. St. Louis, Mo.: Institute for Peace and Justice, and Bloomington, Ind.: Meyer-Stone Books, 1989.

Helping Kids Care: Harmony-Building Activities for Home, Church, and School, by Camy Condon and James McGinnis. St. Louis, Mo.: Institute for Peace and Justice, and Bloomington, Ind.: Meyer-Stone Books, 1988.

Make a World of Difference: Creative Activities for Global Learning, from Church World Service, PO Box 968, Elkhart, IN 46515-0968.

Prepare for Peace: A Peace Study for Children (Part I: Grades 1-3; Part II: Grades 4-6; Part III: Grades 7-8), by Ruth Obold. Newton, Kan.: Faith & Life Press, 1986.

Young Peacemakers Project Book, by Kathleen Fry-Miller, Judith Myers-Walls, and Janet R. Domey-Shenk (vol. 2). 2 vols. Elgin, Ill.: Brethren Press, 1988-89.

Youth (and up)

Joining the Army That Sheds No Blood, by Susan Clemmer Steiner. Scottdale, Pa.: Herald Press, 1982, 1991.

Questions that Refuse to Go Away: Peace and Justice in North America, by Marian C. Franz. Scottdale, Pa.: Herald Press, 1991.

Adults

And Who Is My Neighbor? Poverty, Privilege, and the Gospel of Christ, by Gerald W. Schlabach. Scottdale, Pa.: Herald Press, 1990.

Called to Be Peacemakers, by John K. Stoner. New Call to Peacemaking, Box 500, Akron, PA 17501, 1992.

Children of Peace, by J. R. Burkholder and John Bender. Adult Foundation Series quarterly. Scottdale, Pa.: Mennonite Publishing House, 1982.

Why Settle for More and Miss the Best? by Tom Sine. Waco, Tex.: Word Books, 1987; rev. as *Live It Up!* Scottdale, Pa.: Herald Press, 1993.

Detailed CO Information

Central Committee for Consciencious Objectors (CCCO), 2208 South St., Philadelphia, PA 19146 (215 545-4626). Western Region, P.O. Box 422249, San Francisco, CA 94142 (415 474-3002).

Mennonite Central Committee (MCC), 21 S. 12th St., PO Box 500, Akron, PA 17501-0500 (717 859-1151).

National Interreligious Service Board for Conscientious Objectors (NISBCO), Suite 750, 1601 Connecticut Ave. NW, Washington, DC 20009-1035 (202 483-4510).

Ecology

Cherish the Earth, by Janice and Donald Kirk. Scottdale, Pa.: Herald Press, 1993.

Earth Care News, United Nations Environment Programme, Room DC2-803, United Nations, New York, NY 10017.

Earthkeepers: Environmental Perspectives on Hunger,
    Poverty, and Injustice, by Art and Jocele Meyer. Scottdale,
    Pa.: Herald Press, 1991.
Eco-Church: An Action Manual, by Albert Fritsch, S.J., with
    Angela Iadavaia-Cox. ASPI Publications, R 5, Box 423,
    Livingston, KY 40445.
The Interfaith Coalition on Energy, PO Box 26577,
    Philadelphia, PA 19141 (215 635-1122).
MCC, 21 S. 12th St., PO Box 500, Akron, PA 17501-0500 (717
    859-1151).
101 Ways to Help Save the Earth: With 52 Weeks of
    Congregational Activities to Save the Earth. Eco-Justice
    Working Group, National Council of Churches of Christ,
    475 Riverside Drive, New York, NY 10115 (212 870-2483).
What on Earth Can You Do? by Paula Lehman. Scottdale, Pa.:
    Herald Press, 1993.

Hunger/Responsible Living:
Bread for the World, 802 Rhode Island Ave. NE, Washington,
    DC 20018 (202 269-0200). Christians lobbying for nation-
    al and international hunger issues.
Church World Service, CROP, Box 968, Elkhart, IN 46515 (219
    264-3102).
Living More with Less, by Doris Janzen Longacre. Scottdale,
    Pa.: Herald Press, 1980; *Study/Action Guide,* 1981.

Peace Pole
3534 Lanham Road, Maple City, MI 49664 (616 334-4567).
    Many congregations have placed the pole, which
    proclaims "May Peace Prevail on Earth," in front of their
    building as a symbol of their desire for peace.

Peace Tax Fund Bill
U.S. Peace Tax Fund, 2121 Decatur Pl. NW, Washington, DC
    20008 (202 483-3751).

Plays

Peaceful Heroes, 2 vols. by Rosalie Regen. Westchester, Pa.: Philadelphia Yearly Meeting of the Religious Society of Friends, 1988 reprint.

Swords into Plowshares: A Collection of Plays About Peace and Social Justice, by Ingrid Rogers. Elgin, Ill.: Brethren Press, 1983.

Worship Resources

Mennonite Peace Sunday: Mennonite Board of Congregational Ministries, Box 1245, Elkhart, IN 46515-1245. Provides yearly ideas and helps.

Peace with Justice Week, 475 Riverside Drive, Room 712, New York, NY 10115. Publishes an Organizers Booklet with many resources.

World Food Day, 1001 22nd St. NW, Washington, DC 20437 (202 653-2404). World Food Day is October 16.

The Challenge of the Disciplined Life, by Richard J. Foster. New York: HarperCollins, 1989.

Peace Education: Ideas That Work, from MCC U.S. Peace and Justice Ministries, PO Box 500, Akron, PA 17501-0500.

Peacemaking Through Worship, produced by the Presbyterian Peacemaking Program of the Presbyterian Church, USA. Room 3206, 100 Witherspoon St., Louisville, KY 40202-1396.

Peace Prayers: Meditations, Affirmations, Invocations, Poems and Prayers for Peace, edited by Carrie Leadingham, Jo-ann E. Moschella, and Hilary M. Vartanian (San Francisco: Harper San Francisco, 1992.

Preaching on Peace, edited by Ronald J. Sider and Darrel J. Brubaker. Philadelphia, Pa.: Fortress Press, 1982, 1983.

Also see Bibliography.

Notes

Introduction

1. Quoted by Laura J. Loewen in *Weathering the Storm: Christian Pacifist Response to War*, ed. by Susan Janzen (Faith & Life Press, 1991), 138-139.

2. *Seeds of Peace: A Catalogue of Quotations*, ed. by Jeanne Larson and Madge Micheels-Cyrus. (Philadelphia: New Society Publishers, 1987), 221.

3. The original is in the collection of Associated Mennonite Biblical Seminaries, Elkhart, Indiana, and reproduced here by permission of the artist, Elizabeth Wenger.

Session 1: *Jesus Came to Bring Peace*

1. Quoted by Ronice E. Branding, *Peacemaking: The Journey from Fear to Love* (St. Louis, Mo.: Division of Christian Board of Publication, 1987), 16.

2. This invites discussion between the youth and adult. For more ideas, see the Introduction for Youth and for Adults.

3. *Seeds of Peace*, 106.

4. *Peacemaking Through Worship* (Louisville, Ky.: Presbyterian Peacemaking Program of the Presbyterian Church, USA, n.d.), 47; used by permission.

5. Branding, 72.

6. Susan Clemmer Steiner, *Joining the Army That Sheds No Blood* (Scottdale, Pa.: Herald Press, 1982, 1991), 36.

7. Alan Paton, *Instrument of Thy Peace*, 2nd ed. (London: Wm. Collins PLC, Fount Paperback, 1983); used by permission.

8. First draft of "Inter-Mennonite Confession of Faith," commentary of article on "Peace, Justice, and Nonresistance" (Mar. 28, 1992), lines 1076-1081.

9. First draft of "Inter-Mennonite Confession of Faith," commentary of article on "Peace, Justice, and Nonresistance," lines 1082-1105.

10. *Seeds of Peace*, 162.

11. Dorothy Day, quoted in Steiner, 65.

12. Thanks to Ray Gingerich for counsel on this.

13. *Seeds of Peace*, 146.

14. *The Complete Writings of Menno Simons*, ed. by J. C. Wenger (Scottdale, Pa.: Herald Press, 1956, 1984), 93-94, 198, 200. The composite quotation is available as a poster from Mennonite Central Committee, Akron, Pa.

15. Adapted by Susan Mark Landis and Nancy Ryan Nussbaum from Cornelia Lehn, *Peace Be with You* (Newton, Kan.: Faith & Life Press, 1980), 43-44; used by permission.

16. Cornelius J. Dyck, ed., *An Introduction to Mennonite History* (Scottdale, Pa.: Herald Press, 1967, 1981), 112.

Session 2: *God's Children Love Enemies*

1. *Seeds of Peace*, 163.

2. *Seeds of Peace*, 147.

3. Morton Kelsey, *Caring: How Can We Love One Another?* (Mahway, N.J.: Paulist Press, 1981), 155-168.

4. *Seeds of Peace*, 147.

5. *On Fire for Christ* (Scottdale, Pa.: Herald Press, 1989), 19-24 (about *Martyrs Mirror*), 33-39 ("Between Ice and Fire"); used by permission.

6. *Seeds of Peace*, 197.

Session 3: *We Trust God Alone*

1. F. F. Bruce, *The Spreading Flame* (Grand Rapids: Eerdmans, 1959), 135-146, 176-187; Roland H. Bainton, *the Church of Our Fathers* (New York, N.Y.: Charles Scribner's Sons, 1944), 10-19; see illustrations in Thieleman J. van Braght, *Martyrs Mirror* (Scottdale, Pa.: Herald Press, 1950 translation of the 1660 Dutch original ed.), 106 and other pages.

2. These ideas on worship are from Jim Wallis, "The Meaning of Worship," in *My People, I Am Your Security: Worship Resources in a Nuclear Age* (Washington, D.C.: Sojourners, 1982), 5-6.

3. Ideas in this section are from "Being with the Lamb," by Richard Mouw, in *My People, I Am Your Security*, 34-35.

4. Branding, 56.

5. *Peace Prayers: Meditations, Affirmations, Invocations, Poems and Prayers for Peace*, ed. by Carrie Leadingham, Joann E. Moschella, and Hilary M. Vartanian (San Francisco: Harper San Francisco, 1992), 76.

6. John K. Stoner, "Nine to Five," *Gospel Herald*, April 7, 1987, 236.

7. *Seeds of Peace*, 184.

8. Steiner, 61.

9. *Seeds of Peace*, 106.

10. Ray H. Abrams, *Preachers Present Arms* (New York: Round Table Press, 1933; Scottdale, Pa.: Herald Press, 1969).

11. *Seeking Peace* (Intercourse, Pa.: Good Books, 1991), 21-24; used by permission; adapted from J. Georg Ewert, "Christ or Country?" *The Plough* (May 1984): 6-10.

Session 4: *Peace Is God's Vision*

1. Points *a* to *c* condensed from *Children of Peace*, by J. R. Burkholder and John Bender (Elgin, Ill.: Brethren Press; Nappanee, Ind.: Evangel Press; Newton, Kan.: Faith & Life Press; Scottdale, Pa.: Mennonite Publishing House, 1982), 22-24; point *d* is from Ray Gingerich, note of Nov. 21, 1992.

2. *Peacemaker's Journal.*

3. *Peacemaking Through Worship*, 52; used by permission.

4. Suad Wakim Kesler, in a letter to Jim and Kathy McGinnis.

5. Elizabeth Weaver Kreider, *A Christian Peacemaker's Journal* (Intercourse, Pa.: Good Books, 1991).

6. Peter Copeland, "Researcher Lists 14 Wars Fought in 1991," *The South Bend Tribune*, Dec. 29, 1991, from the Scripps Howard News Service.

7. *Peacemaking Through Worship*, 52; used by permission.

8. Abrams, 68.

9. *Peace Be with You*, 22-23; used by permission.

Session 5: *God Created All Peoples*

1. Reported by Dorothy Nation, *Women of Courage,* as quoted in *Seeds of Peace,* 112.

2. *Seeds of Peace,* 105.

3. *Seeds of Peace,* 112.

4. Kathleen and James McGinnis, *Parenting for Peace and Justice.* (Maryknoll, N.Y.: Orbis, 1981), 60.

5. *Seeds of Peace,* 101.

6. New York: Doubleday, 1980.

7. Condensed from their handout "What to Do About Racism?"

8. UNICEF's answer: butter from New Zealand, coconuts from the Philippines, trucks from Japan, paper from Canada, sugar from Ecuador, ship from the USSR, peanuts from the Sudan, corn syrup from the USA, cocoa from Ghana, and the chocolate bar itself from Great Britain.

9. *Seeds of Peace,* 114.

10. For the thoughts on the atonement that follow, I thank Lois Barrett, personal letter; and John Driver, *Understanding the Atonement for the Mission of the Church* (Scottdale, Pa.: Herald Press, 1986), 226-229.

11. *Seeds of Peace,* 259.

12. *They Loved Their Enemies* (Scottdale, Pa.: Herald Press, 1988), 50-53; used with permission.

Session 6: *We Make Peace*

1. Charles Clements, *Witness to War: An American Doctor in El Salvador* (New York: Bantam, 1984), as quoted in *Seeds of Peace,* 128.

2. *Seeds of Peace,* 211.

3. *Reweaving the Web of Life: Feminism and Nonviolence,* ed. by Pam McAllister (Philadelphia: New Society Pubs., 1982), as quoted in *Seeds of Peace,* 261.

4. Ammon Hennacy, quoted in *Seeds of Peace,* 74.

5. The idea is from St. Augustine, as paraphrased by Branding, 41.

6. These points are condensed from Branding, 65-68.

7. Check these passages for information about early church business meetings, with loud differences of opinion: Acts 6:1-6; 11:1-18; 15:1-35; 15:36-41.

8. See Romans 12:18; 14:19; 1 Thessalonians 5:13.

9. *Seeds of Peace*, 209.

10. *Seeds of Peace*, 215.

11. James McGinnis, *Journey into Compassion: A Spirituality for the Long Haul* (New York: Meyer-Stone Books, 1989), 5.

12. As in *Hymnal: A Worship Book* (Elgin, Ill.: Brethren Press; Newton, Kan.: Faith & Life Press; Scottdale, Pa.: Mennonite Publishing House, 1992), 733; used by permission.

13. Condensed from McGinnis, *Journey*, 128-130.

14. Branding, 71.

15. *Coals of Fire* (Scottdale, Pa.: Herald Press, 1954, 1982), 55-58; used by permission.

16. *Seeds of Peace*, 211.

Appendix 1: *Family Peace Education*

1. Kevin Ryan, *Questions and Answers on Moral Education*, A Fastback Title (Bloomington, Ind.: Phi Delta Kappa Educational Foundation, 1981).

2. *The Way of Peace* (Scottdale, Pa.: Herald Press, 1977), 36.

3. *Peacemaker's Journal*.

4. From her gem of a book, *Gently Lead: How to Teach Your Children About God While Finding Out for Yourself* (New York: Harper Collins, 1991), 65. While Berends is unabashedly Christian, she unapologetically draws ideas from other religions.

5. From Doug Penner, "War, Peace, and the Workplace," in *Weathering the Storm*, ed. by Susan E. Janzen (Newton, Kan.: Faith & Life Press, 1991), 88.

6. Nancy Carlsson-Paige and Diane E. Levin, *Who's Calling the Shots: How to Respond Effectively to Children's Fascination with War Play and War Toys* (Philadelphia: New Society Pubs., 1990).

7. *Peacemaker's Journal*.

8. MCC's U.S. address is 21 S. 12th Street, P.O. Box 500, Akron, PA 17501-0500; and in Canada, 134 Plaza Dr., Winnipeg, MB R3T 5K9.

9. Doris Janzen Longacre, *More-with-Less Cookbook*, commissioned by Mennonite Central Committee in response to world food needs (Scottdale, Pa.: Herald Press, 1976), with about three-fourths of a million in print and still available; and *Living More with Less* (Scottdale, Pa.: Herald Press, 1980).

10. *Seeds of Peace*, 107.
11. From his speech at Laurelville, Feb. 6, 1988.
12. *Seeds of Peace*, 206.
13. *Seeds of Peace*, 210.

Appendix 4: *Congregational Peace Education*
1. Contact Ohio Conference, PO Box 210, Kidron, OH 44636 (216 857-5421) for information about their Peace Trunk of books which visits congregations.

Youth Reading List

(For aid with this list, thanks to Christian Peace Elf, a reading program of Kingview Mennonite Church, Scottdale, Pa. Books are from Herald Press unless otherwise noted.)

Session 1

Kauffmann, Joel. *The Weight.* 1980.

> A preacher's son tries to decide if he is a CO during the Vietnam War. Also available on videotape from Sisters and Brothers, 1251 Va. Ave., Harrisonburg, VA 22801.

De Kay, James T. *Meet Martin Luther King.* New York: Random, 1969.

> This story of Martin Luther King, Jr. includes photos.

Speare, Elizabeth G. *The Bronze Bow.* Boston: Houghton Mifflin, 1961.

> Daniel Bar Jamin's contact with Jesus transforms his life.

Vernon, Louise A. *A Heart Strangely Warmed.* 1975.

> Two boys become acquainted with John Wesley, who helped start the Methodist Church.

Vernon, Louise A. *Night Preacher.* 1969.

> Menno Simon's children, Bettje and Jan, tell their father's story.

Session 2

Brink, Carol R. *Caddie Woodlawn.* New York: Macmillan
    Children's Bk. Group, 1973.
    A "tomboy" on the Wisconsin frontier befriends a local
    native American, and tries to keep her people from hurting
    his people.

Creighton, Jill and Robert. *The Weaver's Horse.* Buffalo: Firefly
    Bks. 1991.
    Lord Henry, a warrior, chooses "to be done with fighting"
    and becomes a weaver.

Dyck, Peter J. *The Great Shalom,* and *Shalom at Last.* 1990-92.
    As animals in the forest try to stop the farmer from cutting
    down their trees, readers discover how to deal with
    conflict.

Eitzen, Ruth and Allan. *The White Feather.* 1987.
    A white family makes peace with Native Americans.

Erickson, Russel. *Toad for Tuesday.* New York: Lothrop, 1974.
    A charming tale about how a toad, being saved for an owl's
    lunch, wins the owl's friendship.

Jackson, Dave and Neta. *On Fire for Christ.* 1989.
    These Christians preferred to die rather than renounce
    their beliefs in Jesus. Fifteen stories from *Martyrs Mirror.*

Vernon, Louise A. *The Christmas Surprise.* 1989.
    Wonders happen in Bethlehem, Pennsylvania, during the
    French and Indian War.

Session 3

Collier, James Lincoln and Christopher. *My Brother Sam Is
    Dead.* New York: Macmillan Children's Bk. Group, 1977.
    Based-on-fact book about stress in the American
    Revolution.

Giblin, James C. *Walls: Defenses Throughout History.* Boston:
    Little, Brown, & Co., 1984.
    Barriers like the Berlin wall fail to keep enemies out.

Giff, Patricia. *Mother Teresa.* New York: Viking Children's Bks.,
    1986.

Called the Saint of Calcutta, Mother Teresa cares for the starving and homeless.

Schloneger, Florence E. *Sara's Trek.* Newton, Kan.: Faith & Life, 1982.

A girl is separated from her refugee family during World War II.

Smucker, Barbara Classen. *Days of Terror.* 1979.

The government in Russia changes, creating frightening experiences for a family.

Smucker, Barbara. *Henry's Red Sea.* 1955.

Refugees depend on God to save them.

Session 4

Avi. *The Fighting Ground.* New York: Harper Collins Children's Books, 1987.

One day in the life of Jonathan, a Revolutionary War 13-year-old, his view of war changes.

Langton, Jean. *The Fragile Flag.* New York: Harper Collins Children's Bks., 1989.

Uncle Freddie's flag takes a 450-mile pilgrimage after Georgie hears about the "Peace Missile."

Mattingly, Christobel. *The Miracle Tree.* San Diego: Harcourt Brace Janovich, 1986.

Perhaps even the terrible atomic tragedy that blasted Japan can be overcome.

Merrill, Jean. *The Pushcart War.* New York: Harper Collins Children's Bks., 1964.

Competition on the streets of New York City provides inspiration for this imaginative tale.

Session 5

Cameron, Ann. *The Most Beautiful Place in the World.* New York: Alfred A. Knopf, 1988.

Juan shares his life growing up in Guatemala.

Frank, Anne. *Anne Frank: The Diary of a Young Girl.* New York: Doubleday, 1967.

Through Anne's eyes we understand the everyday
experiences of Jews hiding during World War II.

Griffin, John H. *Black Like Me.* New York: NAL Dutton, 1962.
A white man colors his skin black to experience prejudice
in the South firsthand.

Jacobs, Francine. *The Tainos: The People Who Welcomed
Columbus.* New York: Putnam Publishing Group, 1992.
Columbus and later Europeans enslaved the Tainos to
satisfy Europe's gold-hunger. Christian missionaries
provide us with a prophetic example.

Martin, Bill, Jr., and John Archambault. *Knots on a Counting
Rope.* New York: Henry Nolt, 1987.
With the help of his grandfather, a Native American boy
faces the biggest obstacle in his life—his blindness.

Meltzer, Milton. *Mary McLeod Bethune: Voice of Black Hope.*
New York: Viking Children's Books, 1987.
The granddaughter of Africans brought to North America
as slaves, Mary McLeod Bethune is born into freedom.

Ralston, Sonia. *Plowshares: A Contemporary Fable of Peace
and War.* Mahwah, N.J.: Paulist Press, 1986.
A mother helps two fighting groups start to work together.

Rocha, Ruth, and Otavio Roth. *The Universal Declaration of
Human Rights: An Adaptation for Children.* New York:
United Nations, 1992.
Basic but moving truths communicated in plain language.

Sebastyen, Ouida. *Words by Heart.* New York: Bantam, 1983.
A young African-American learns that winning a Scripture
memory contest may not overcome racial prejudices.

Session 6

Ferris, Jeri. *Walking the Road to Freedom: A Story about
Sojourner Truth.* Minneapolis: Lerner Pubns., 1989.
The true story of an African-American woman orator who
spoke out against slavery.

Lowry, Lois. *Number the Stars.* New York: Dell, 1990.

Annemarie and her family protect Ellen Rosen and other Jews in Denmark during World War II.

Moore, Ruth Nulton. *Distant Thunder.* 1991.

Fifteen-year-old Kate and her friends show how Moravians can help the suffering in the American Revolution.

Naidoo, Beverly. *Journey to Jo'burg.* New York: Harper Collins Children's Bks., 1986.

Thirteen-year-old Naledi and her nine-year-old brother, Tiro, travel by themselves through 300 kilometers of South African countryside to save their baby sister.

Sterling, Dorothy. *Freedom Train.* New York: Scholastic Inc., 1987.

A biography of Harriet Tubman, who escaped from slavery, then led others along the same "underground railroad."

Bibliography

(Numbers in parentheses indicate related sessions. Books are from Herald Press unless otherwise indicated.)

(1) Bainton, Roland H. *Christian Attitudes Toward War and Peace.* Nashville: Abingdon Press, 1988.

(4) Barrett, Lois. *The Way God Fights: War and Peace in the Old Testament.* 1987.

Bauman, Elizabeth Hershberger. *Coals of Fire.* 1954, 1982.

(4) Boers, Arthur Paul. *On Earth as in Heaven: Justice Rooted in Spirituality.* 1991.

Braght, Thieleman J. van. *Martyrs Mirror.* 1938 (still in print).

Branding, Ronice E. *Peacemaking: The Journey from Fear to Love.* St. Louis, Mo.: Division of Christian Board of Publication, 1987.

Burkholder, J. R., and John Bender. *Children of Peace.* Scottdale, Pa.: Mennonite Publishing House et al.; 1982.

(4) Byler, Dennis. *Making War and Making Peace: Why Some Christians Fight and Some Don't.* 1989.

Carlsson-Paige, Nancy, and Diane E. Levin. *Who's Calling the Shots? How to Respond Effectively to Children's Fascination with War Play and War Toys.* Philadelphia: New Society Pubns., 1990.

(6) Classen, Susan. *Vultures and Butterflies: Living the Contradictions.* 1992.

Copeland, Peter. "Researcher Lists 14 Wars Fought in 1991." Washington, D.C.: Scripps Howard News Service, Dec. 29, 1991 (*South Bend Tribune*).

Dear, John. *Disarming the Heart*. Rev. ed. 1993.

Donaghy, John A. *Peacemaking and the Community of Faith: A Handbook for Congregations*. Ramsey, N.J.: Paulist Press, 1983.

Drescher, John. *Why I Am a Conscientious Objector*. 1982.

Driver, John. *How Christians Made Peace with War: Early Christian Understandings of War*. 1988.

_____. *Understanding the Atonement for the Mission of the Church*. 1986.

(4) Eller, Vernard. *War and Peace from Genesis to Revelation*. 1981.

(3) Franz, Marian. *Questions that Refuse to Go Away: Peace and Justice in North America*. 1991.

Friesen, Ivan and Rachel. *Shalom Pamphlets*. 1981.

(3) Grimsrud, Ted. *Triumph of the Lamb: A Self-Study Guide to the Book of Revelation*. 1987.

(5) Gwyn, Douglas, George Hunsinger, Eugene F. Roop, and John H. Yoder. *A Declaration on Peace: In God's People the World's Renewal Has Begun*. 1990.

Hostetler, Marian. *They Loved Their Enemies: True Stories of African Christians*. 1988.

(2) Jackson, Dave and Neta. *On Fire for Christ: Stories of Anabaptist Martyrs Retold from Martyrs Mirror*. 1989.

Janzen, Waldemar. *Still in the Image*. Institute of Mennonite Studies Series, no. 6. Newton, Kan.: Faith & Life Press, 1982.

(3) Kehler, Larry. *The Rule of the Lamb*. Newton, Kan.: Faith & Life Press, 1978.

Kraybill, Donald B. *The Upside-Down Kingdom*. Scottdale, Pa.: Herald Press, 1978.

(4) Lind, Millard C. *Yahweh Is a Warrior*. 1980.

(3) Lord, Charlie. *The Rule of the Sword*. Newton, Kan.: Faith & Life Press, 1978.

McGinnis, James. *Journey into Compassion: A Spirituality for the Long Haul*. Bloomington, Ind.: Meyer-Stone Books; St. Louis, Mo.: The Institute for Peace and Justice; 1989.

Martin, Maurice. *Identity and Faith: Youth in a Believer's Church*. 1981.

My People, I Am Your Security. Washington, D.C.: Sojourners, 1982.

Oyer, John S., and Robert S. Kreider. *Mirror of the Martyrs*. Intercourse, Pa.: Good Books, 1990.

Peachey, J. Lorne. *How to Teach Peace to Children.* 1981.

Peachey, Titus and Linda Gehman. *Seeking Peace.* Intercourse, Pa.: Good Books, 1991.

Roth, Willard, Editor. *Peacemaker Pamphlets.* 1964.

(2) Ruth-Heffelbower, Duane. *The Anabaptists Are Back! Making Peace in a Dangerous World.* 1991.

Ryan, Kevin. *Questions and Answers on Moral Education.* Bloomington, Ind.: Phi Delta Kappa Educational Foundation, 1981.

(6) Schlabach, Gerald W. *And Who Is My Neighbor? Poverty, Privilege, and the Gospel of Christ.* 1990.

(2) Sider, Ronald J. *Christ and Violence.* 1979.

_____. *Nonviolence: The Invincible Weapon?* Dallas: Word Publishing, 1989.

Steiner, Susan Clemmer. *Joining the Army That Sheds No Blood.* 1982, 1991.

Stoner, John K., and Lois Barrett. *Letters to American Christians.* 1989.

Wenger, J. C. *The Way of Peace.* 1977.

(1) Yoder, John Howard. *He Came Preaching Peace.* 1985.

_____. *Nevertheless: Varieties of Religious Pacifism.* Rev. and expanded ed. 1992.

(1) _____. *The Original Revolution: Essays on Christian Pacifism.* 1971, 1977.

(1) _____. *The Politics of Jesus.* Grand Rapids, Mich.: William B. Eerdmans Publishing Company, 1972.

(2) _____. *What Would You Do?* Expanded ed. 1992.

(4) Yoder, Perry. *Shalom: The Bible's Word for Salvation, Justice, and Peace.* Newton, Kan.: Faith & Life Press, 1987.

Scripture Index

Evaluation Form

To aid in planning future projects, please photocopy this sheet, answer the questions, and mail to the address given. Thanks!

1. What went well as you used the book? How did it help you and your child grow?

2. What about the book was frustrating? What should be changed?

3. What ideas about family or congregational peace education do you want to pass along?

Add any additional comments and mail with your youth's response to Susan Mark Landis, c/o Herald Press, 616 Walnut Ave., Scottdale, PA 15683.

The Author

Susan Mark Landis was born in Santa Fe, New Mexico, while her father did alternate service in I-W during the Korean War. She early embraced conscientious objection. Susan remembers looking around her fourth-grade classroom and wondering which of her classmates would be wasted in the Vietnam War. Susan's mother, to keep their peace beliefs strong, organized peace retreats for the youth of her home congregation, Prairie Street, in Elkhart, Indiana.

When grown, Susan helped plan intergenerational peace retreats for her present congregation, Oak Grove Mennonite, Smithville, Ohio. In the Ohio Conference of the Mennonite Church, she is active as a peace and justice educator and as Peace-Justice-Service Commission chairperson. She offers her peace workshops and retreats to the wider church through the Mennonite Board of Congregational Ministries, Elkhart, by serving as a Partner-at-Large.

Landis is in a Master of Peace Arts program at Associated Mennonite Biblical Seminaries, Elkhart. This book grew out of her stimulating classes and friendships there.

Her joys include parenting grade-schoolers Laura and Joel with Dennis, her husband, an English teacher, librarian, curriculum consultant, and computer technician at Central Christian High School, Kidron, Ohio. Baking bread, reading aloud with the children, and creating family celebrations are pleasant extras in her family life. The Landis home is in Orrville, Ohio.